IS YOUR SOUL ON LIFE SUPPORT?

You Are Meant to Be Well

Mary Gasa Ph.D

Cover Design by 100Covers.com
Interior Design by FormattedBooks.com

Thank you for picking up a copy of this book. I sincerely hope that it will be of benefit to you as you seek healing and growth.

There is a FREE gift for you to help you on your journey. Go to Turray Productions on facebook and claim your FREE workbook to help you track your journey to wellness.

Dedication

This dedicated first to my dear Lord, without who's direction and inspiration, this book would not have been possible.

My loving and patient husband, George. His continued encouragement and belief in me have kept me going. I love you for all eternity

Donna Hanlon, one of my dearest friends, whom I hope to meet in person one day, and give a big hug to. She has laughed and cried with me and always given me encouragement. She is the only one of my friends who told me that I could do this.

Contents

Part I

Part II

Part III

Part I

Introduction

WHY YOU OR A LOVED One Will Benefit from This Book.

Oh, goody! Another self-help book. You may be saying to yourself, "What makes this one any different?" The question you should be asking is, "Does this book give me some of the answers and guidance I have been seeking?"

I say this because each book is written from a particular expert's viewpoint. Each of them has value, but which one has the answers that your personal needs and situation require? It has been said that each of us is an angel with answers. In that sense, each expert is an angel. Your mission is to find the angel with the answers or direction you need.

Let's take a look at where you are and what you are seeking. Wouldn't you agree that you need a starting point to know how to proceed? Do any of the following statements come close to you and what you are looking for?

Do you have days or weeks when you find yourself just dragging and trying to go through the motions? You tell yourself that it is just the season or the workload you are under. But it is more than that.

You work at eating healthy, lots of salads and little to no junk food. The idea of enjoying a meal is a thing of the past, because you are watching every bite, calorie, and gram of fat or carbs.

Exercise makes you more tired and discouraged. You are worn out before you even begin.

You feel trapped in a personal or professional situation that is unhealthy for you. What can you do?

You are at a point in your life where you realize that things just have not worked out the way you had hoped, planned, or prayed that they would.

You are at a loss and searching for direction, and hopefully a way to change yourself and your situation.

Does any of this strike a chord or sound familiar?

You, my friend, are suffering from one or more forms of dis- ease. "Dis-ease" being defined as a lack of ease, or any condition or tendency that is regarded as harmful. You may try to ignore this, but that does not make it go away.

Ignoring a problem allows it time to grow and fester within. This will ultimately only make it harder to solve.

You may be caring for your physical body, and even your mental fitness level. Have you taken time to even think about the third part of your being, your spirit or soul? Sometimes that bone-weary feeling that leaves you just wanting to find a safe corner and stay there is your spirit telling you that it needs rest and some serious TLC.

You may wonder what I am talking about or why it is even that important. Proverbs 18:14 tells us, "The spirit of man will sustain his infirmity, but a wounded spirit who can bear?" This is an example of the importance of the spirit to your overall wellbeing. The spirit/soul can handle it if the body is ill or injured. It can go on. Your body does not do well when the spirit is injured.

Physical fatigue and spiritual fatigue may at first appear to be two separate things, but they are very strongly interconnected. As the pre-ceding scripture indicates, the spirit and body are so intertwined that they strongly affect each other. This explains why you feel so physically drained after going through an emotional time. It is not your physical body that is crying for rest and recovery, it is your spirit/soul. To con-tinue to ignore the soul's pleas for help is to your own peril.

You may ask why you should listen to me. What gives me the author-ity to suggest how to help your situation?

While I have been very blessed in this life, it has not always been easy. Like many, I have not always made wise choices. I dropped out of high school to marry the father of my baby. I did manage to earn my GED between having babies. After a decade of physical and mental abuse and betrayal, I survived a nasty divorce. I had been a stay at home mom, and now I was dumped into the reality of trying to find employ-ment while learning to reinvent myself or find what my purpose was. There were times when I felt as if parts of me were being torn apart and stomped into the ground. After being released from several dead-end jobs, I managed to start business school. There, they helped me find a good part-time job.

My children were being shuffled between my house and their father's. Not an optimal situation. One day, I had to rush my six-year-old son to the hospital with a hot appendix that burst as they got him on the operating table. He made it through but was a sick little boy and required a second surgery to drain an infection. He was hospitalized for a month. A week or so later, his younger sister ran out in front of a car and wound up with a broken leg. She needed to be in traction for four weeks and a cast that went from just under her arm pits, all the way down her injured leg. My two youngest in the hospital at the same time. What a way to spend a summer.

In the fall, my dear mother passed away. She had been an emotional rock for me when everything else was slipping from my grasp. A few weeks after her passing, I came home to find four fire engines in front of my home. There had been a fire that gutted one room and left smoke damage throughout. Talk about feeling like getting hit in the gut with a ten-pound sledge. My body and soul were too numb to even cry.

I am relating all of this to show you that I have been in some hurtful situations and have learned how injured the soul can become.

One of many things that I have learned is that even when you feel the most alone, you are not if you just reach up and ask for help and guidance. Another lesson has been that while the body may seem to have recovered, the soul is still gasping and struggling to survive.

There are three levels of our being that need care and attention: the body, the mind and the soul or spirit.

As I have looked around, I have found all sorts of books on helping the body stay fit or to rebuild. Eat this. Don't eat that. Follow this exercise routine and find a new you. Some work for a little while and others just leave you exhausted and discouraged, feeling more like a failure than you already did.

There are books and seminars to help you learn to change how you think and look at life. Read this book and change the whole world. Once upon a time you were instructed to listen to these subliminal tapes or CD's while you slept. That has moved onto positive affirmations recited every morning and night and anytime in between. Retrain your thinking and outlook. Good in theory, but seldom works well in the real world.

There are not a lot of books that address the care and healing of the spirit or soul. That is why I have felt compelled to write and share this book with you. It is important to heal on all levels, to find the strength and balance that you are seeking.

I promise that if you read and use what is shared in this book, you will find healing for your soul and new strength and purpose in your life.

As a child of God, healing
belongs to you.

Chapter I

Identifying the Problem

WILL THIS BOOK GIVE ME Some of the Answers and Guidance That I am Looking for?

There are many, many books and articles that offer help and healing. They give you guidelines on how to heal, rebuild and transform your body into a whole new you. Some work for some people, and some do not work at all.

How do you go about recognizing which of these materials and messages are what you need? Here are a couple of suggestions. Is the message something new to you, or does it come from a direction you had not thought of? Does it strike a certain note deep within you? Are you drawn to read more?

Sometimes when a person is beginning a healing journey, it can be nice to invite a friend to accompany them; like a 'buddy system'. When the going gets rough, they are there to encourage. You might consider someone you would like to share this with.

Let us look at where you are and what you are hoping for. Wouldn't you agree that you need a starting point to know how to proceed?

We covered a lot of the situations in the introduction, but let's recap a little

Do you feel like you are just going through the motions, like you are on autopilot? It may seem as if you are in a stupor or on an endless merry-go-round.

No matter how much sleep you get, you still feel exhausted. Even coffee and vitamins or energy drinks don't help.

Everyone tells you that you are just out of shape and that by getting on their fabulous new exercise program you will feel better and have more energy. Right. You try and all you get is discouraged and more tired. Deep down you are starting to feel like a failure.

You are at a point in your life where you are starting to feel as if life has passed you by. This is not what you had envisioned.

Your health and/or your weight are not where you feel they should be. Just look at everyone else. They make looking good seem so effortless.

Do you feel trapped in a in a private or professional situation that is unhealthy for you? How did you get there? What did you do to deserve it? No matter how much you would like to, you can't leave. How would you manage without it? The benefits are too good to quit. You tell yourself all sorts of reasons to stay where you are, but when you get down to it, you know that you need to make some changes. The fear of doing that is making you feel trapped and maybe a little desperate.

Are your children, if you have any, are getting ready to leave the nest, or have they already flown? Or do you have the opposite situation of having one who is more than reluctant to leave the comforts of home. Perhaps the opposite is happening. You have an aged parent who needs to move in with you, because they can no longer manage on their own.

Constantly making excuses has become a habit. It seems easier to make an excuse than to take the blame. Is it really?

Are you at a loss and searching for direction, and hopefully a way to change yourself and your situation? Sometimes you may just wish it would all take care of itself and you would not have to do any more.

There is little fun or joy, because you no longer have the interest or energy for things that used to arouse your passions and bring you pleasure. Who has time for hobbies when just getting through each day is a challenge? When was the last time you really had a good laugh and didn't feel like you had to paste on a smile?

Have you been trying to ignore the symptoms? There just is not time to be ill. The thought of coping with one more thing is beyond you. You can't be or get sick. There is no one to take care of you.

Whatever your reason may be, understand that ignoring a problem does not make it go away. The problem will fester and grow, making things worse and ultimately harder to solve. It may even lead to a serious or life-threatening disorder. It can be like a sliver that gets in your foot. At first, you may not even notice it. Later, your foot may start to hurt some, but you are too busy to take the time to tend to it. Given a little more time, you start to limp, so you call your doctor for an appointment. By the time you finally get in to see him, you have developed a serious infection that requires minor surgery to remove said sliver and drain the infection. After being given a prescription, you are sent home and told to stay off your foot for a few days. You must miss work, and need to be taken care of, all because you ignored the problem in the beginning.

There are any number of articles and books that promise a whole new you. You can transform your life and your body if you will just follow their eating regime and exercise at least three times a week. There are several things wrong with this approach. The first is something that I am only going to cover once. Because of different body and blood types, the same diet and exercise program does not work the same way for everyone. You are not to blame when you do not get the results that were espoused. You are not a failure, so stop beating yourself up.

The second problem is that they only tackle one particular part of the problem instead of treating the whole individual. It is important to realize that you are composed of different parts or levels. You have not been caring for all the levels that you are made up of.

The first level is the obvious, the body. Good nutritious food is consumed. You exercise to try to stay fit and strong, or not. It may feel like another full- time job. Sometimes it is difficult to get motivated, or to find the time to do all the things you are told to do to stay fit.

Then there is the mental level. When was the last time you listened to a podcast or some favorite music? Have you read something non-work related lately, or just relaxed? Do you take any time for any of these, or are you constantly connected to your electronics? You must stay connected so your boss can get ahold of you at all hours. Maybe your kids might need you to come running or to check in where they are. Are you constantly checking to see what is happening online, so you don't miss out on something? Ask yourself if you have become so programmed that you are afraid of being left out of something. Where is your down time to recharge? How much of the real life around you are you missing?

You may be caring for your physical body, even your mind or mental level, but have you thought about your soul or spirit? I do not mean this in the old "Holy Roller" sense—or when was the last time you went to church sort of way—but in the sense that the soul is part of your being and needs your care. Sometimes that bone-weary feeling that leaves you just wanting to find a safe corner and stay there is your spirit telling you that it needs rest and some TLC.

You may wonder why this is so important. The spirit can handle it if the body is ill or injured. It can go on. Your body does not do well when the spirit is injured. The following example may show you some of what I mean.

A few years ago, a person whom I know well was dumped by their own child. They were told that it was no longer healthy to be in a relationship with said young adult. There had been no abuse, neglect, or anything. Four months later, this person was in the hospital with heart problems. They had been healthy up until then. When we talked, the realization that their heart had been broken by this abandonment became very apparent. Their soul had taken a major hit. It was not just the body that needed time to heal. Talking and time helped the spirit to recover. When they took action to help their spirit to heal, their body was able to make a full recovery.

While physical fatigue and emotional fatigue may appear to be two separate things, they are strongly interconnected. The soul and body are so intertwined that they strongly affect each other. This is one of the reasons that you feel so physically drained when you go through an emotional time. It is not only your physical body that is fatigued, but your spiritual one.

My husband recently retired, and we moved to a different home. We had been in our previous home for fifteen years and I was not a particular fan of the place. While I had spent a lot of effort in making it into a home, it just never really felt like one. The move was sudden, and we were not as prepared as we could have been.

While moves are incredibly stressful, this one seemed to drain every last bit of the reserves that I had. It was difficult to come to terms with just how damaged and weary my soul had become. Each day was a challenge to get the things done that we needed, to rest when necessary, and to stop beating myself up for not having the endurance and strength to do more. The harder that I worked, the worse it became. Finally, it became clear that the only way anything was going to get done was if I took the time to take care of myself and let my strength and spirit or soul recuperate.

Any number of things can drain or cause your soul great anguish. It may be something simple, like worrying about things you cannot control to more serious situations.

- Is someone you care about deeply going through a difficult time? You would like to help but haven't found a way.
- Have you gone through a breakup or divorce? You may have been left feeling empty inside and lost. Moving forward is a struggle.
- Did someone or something that you really cared about die? Whether it was a person or a pet, you feel the loss deeply.
- Have you recently applied for a new position? You have not heard back from them. You are in a type of limbo; hoping they might still call or beating yourself up for not getting it.

These are just a few examples of things that can cause soul fatigue.

Let's talk about balance and harmony in our lives. When the soul has taken one too many hits and needs tender care, it could be a sign that you are out of balance with what your true purpose may be.

At one time, I thought that my purpose was to be a good mother, wife and daughter. After years of enduring mental and physical abuse, there was a bitter divorce. I was left feeling lost and bereft. I was in a place that the scriptures refer to as a "wilderness" or a difficult time of suffering. I beat up my already hurting soul with questions of self-doubt and wondered why I wasn't enough. I was filled with anger at both him and myself. There was fear as well. How was I supposed to move forward? Not having a guide to help me with this, it took a few years for me to find my purpose again and redirect.

One of the biggest lessons I learned, is that as you go through life and its different stages, you may find that your purpose changes or shifts. Pay attention to these subtle changes, because when the flow of the soul's energy gets disrupted, the soul weakens and starts to wither. You, in turn, start to feel that drain of energy. You are being told something. Listen. It is important for your wellbeing.

Ask yourself, "How disoriented and lost am I feeling?" Be really honest in your answer. Is it time to stop lying to yourself? If you are genuinely interested in moving forward and healing from within, it is time to make some positive changes in your life.

"Unless commitment is made,
there are only promises and
hope...but no plans."

Peter Drucker

Chapter II

Commitment to Change

LIFE, WITH ITS EVER-EVOLVING TERRAIN, requires us to shift gears or take steps to evolve as well. If you are like most people, the idea of real change can leave you quaking inside, while you hang on the edge of what you know for as long as you can. Change can be very, very scary for some people, even terrifying. Most people only make changes to their lives when the pain of staying the same is greater than the pain of change. Are you there yet?

Harmony and purpose are going to be mentioned a lot. When you have consistently over booked, over scheduled, and overworked yourself, there has been no time for you—no time to breathe, no time to enjoy the moment, no time to recover and recharge. There is an old saying urging us to "keep on doing, because you can rest when you are dead." Is that really when you would choose to rest? You may be so driven that you feel taking a break is a waste of time. In actuality, taking a little time for yourself may be what will help your soul and save you. We were put on this earth so that we might have joy, not work ourselves to a frazzle.

You may have started out with all sorts of plans about what you were going to accomplish and do. You wrote out what you wanted and even made a dream board. You were in charge and great things were in store. Then life came along and smacked you up alongside the head, and it hit harder than you thought it could. You have probably found out by now that some things in life seem to work extremely hard to break you down. Just when you think things are getting better, you get smacked down again. Try not to get discouraged. Most of the time, when you are set on a good work, the adversary will do all he can to stop you. Refocus and go on.

You may be one of those people who never really planned. You just drifted along with the current. You seemed to feel that if you worked hard at doing the right things, everything would be okay. Now, you look around and find out that you had the wrong concept about how life goes. You may feel like the old saying of being like a horse who has been ridden hard and put away wet. (Meaning that you feel worn out and not cared for—maybe even discarded.)

Life does throw curveballs, and even a plan is not set in stone. Constant reevaluations have to be done all the time. Just like me, you may find that your purpose has changed significantly, and you are scrambling to find and identify it again.

Your coworkers and acquaintances may think that you are just going through a rough patch or a mid-life crisis. No one can or is willing to relate to what is troubling you. Worse yet, you cannot find the words to describe or explain it. You just feel lost and depleted. It would be genuinely nice if the world would just go away and let you curl up with your favorite blankey and a quart of chocolate ice cream.

One of the most important things that you absolutely need to understand, is that it is perfectly okay for you to fall apart a little bit for a little while. You do not always have to be the strong one. Give yourself permission to go have a good cry and feel better. Ease up and accept that you do not have to always have it all together. Know that it is OKAY to not be okay all the time.

Do you wonder how you got to this point? Lots of things have led you here. If you are like most of us, you have ignored or misinterpreted the signs that have led you to this point. Trust me, your soul has been trying to get your attention. If you doubt that, let's take a closer look.

Earlier, I mentioned feeling tired all the time. No matter how much you sleep, it is never enough to make you feel rested. I know a person who insists that they need eight to nine hours of sleep a night or they just do not function. He has been this way for many years. After closely observing and conversing with him, it became very apparent that his soul is crying for rest and nourishment. Several things had happened in his past that had seriously wounded his soul deeply.

What has happened in your past that has left you reeling or feeling defeated? It does not have to be something that would be considered earth shaking. It may just be the little everyday things that have piled up to the point where you can barely breathe. You look around and it seems like everyone else is handling things. Why aren't you? You have for so long, and now you have reached a point where you need to just take care of you for a short time.

Our society has convinced us that no matter what happens, we are to just buck up and keep going. If you are like most of us, you do just that, because for one reason or another, you have bought into the idea and convinced yourself that is what you do. Think back to one of those times and try to remember what your inner self was trying to tell you. Maybe it was something about needing to breathe or to take a little time to refocus. Like most, you ignored it and pushed on.

As a child of God, healing
belongs to you.

Chapter III

How to Lighten Your Load

HOW STRONG ARE YOU FEELING right now? Maybe you would say that you're feeling pretty good, all in all. Are you being honest, or are you starting to feel like you are not as strong as you feel you should be or that you once were? Your body just kind of aches most of the time. You exercise, but nothing seems to change except you feel more tired and weak, or maybe you ache even more. If you say anything to your friends or family, they just tell you that it is part of growing older. That is an old rationale, and it is a lie. In reality, for a very long time, you have been carrying a load alone. A load that is much too heavy for you to carry alone any longer.

Regardless of what you have been taught, you really do not have to do everything on your own. You are not meant to. Matthew 11:29 tells us to "Take my yoke upon you, and learn of me, for I am meek and lowly in heart; and ye shall find rest for your souls." Now by taking His yoke upon you, you are sharing that very heavy load with the one who will never leave you. The last part of that verse promises that you will "find rest for your souls." Isn't that what you are ultimately seeking?

You may be saying that you have tried that, and it did not work, or that Jesus does not really care about little ole you. Now, there is one particularly important lesson that I have learned over the years. Pay close attention to this. When you turn something over to the Lord for Him to take care of, you must TOTALLY let go of it. Do not hang onto that one little corner, because you are afraid to let go of all of it, or that He will not do it right. As long as you are hanging onto even the tiniest corner, you are not putting ALL your trust in the Lord. He will take care of you and help to heal your soul. It is part of learning to live a guided life.

One of the hardest things for many to learn is that things may not turn out the way you expected or when you may have wanted them to, but it is always for the best. His will and His way and timing are always the best for us, even when we do not recognize it at first. Learn to truly trust in Him. Whatever your personal trials may be, the Lord is telling you that you are not alone and that he loves you.

There is a short article by Sheila Walsh that I found on Facebook, and I would like to share with you. It is about always feeling that you must be in control. It follows:

> "Be still and know that I am God."
> The original Hebrew root of "Be still" doesn't mean "be quiet"; it means "let go."
> That's very different, don't you think?
> Let go and know that I am God!
> Let go of trying to control your spouse!
> Let go of your worry about your finances!
> Let go of your unforgiveness!
> Let go of your past!
> Let go of what you can't control - and rest in the knowledge that God is in control!"

When you realize that God is there for you, you will be able to move forward with renewed courage.

I might add, let go of all your self-doubts.

"The Lord is in the details of our lives."
Thomas S. Monson

Chapter IV

Depression

YOU HAVE SOME WONDERFUL THOUGHTS and ideas. They might even be very innovative and help people. Why don't you share them? Maybe, like so many times before, when you have tried to share your ideas, people just did not understand what the idea or concept was that you were trying to convey. Did people look at you like you were speaking a foreign language? You remember people looking at you strangely and shaking their heads. Sometimes it has been so hard to express yourself that you have stopped trying, letting your soul take another hit.

With this withdrawal, you may draw inward and develop depression. It feels as if no one cares or is interested in what you think. Then comes the day when you are put into a situation that makes you extremely uncomfortable. You are being called upon to share ideas. It feels as if everyone is staring at you, and you feel trapped. Everything seems to be closing in and you can no longer get your breath. You would like to run and hide. You might panic and do just that. You have just experienced a panic attack.

When you and your soul have endured prolonged periods of fatigue, you will start to notice some differences. Along with the depression, you may experience a lack of motivation, a loss of intuition and maybe a loss of psychic gifts. Panic attacks and anxiety become all too familiar. You find yourself drawn to addictive or obsessive behaviors. If you look around, you will find that you are not alone. Depression seems to be an epidemic these days.

Some people physically ache with the feelings of depression and loneliness. They may have headaches, stomach aches or just not feel right. Sometimes they have dizziness, ringing in the ears and /or blurred vision without any discernible medical reasons. While these symptoms may sound annoying, or alarming, depression really can affect you and your body in some serious ways. Yes, I said your body. Depression is not just a mental issue. It can cause severe, and even life threatening, health issues. It lowers your resistance to infection, making it so much easier to catch whatever is going around.

Your chances of developing heart disease are increased by depression. It has been shown to increase the inflammation in the body, making the body more susceptible to disease, especially heart disease. Yes, you can literally die from a broken heart.

How is your memory? Having little lapses, or does it seem that you are not as sharp as you once were? In 2019, the University of Sussex collected and studied the research from the National Child Developmental Study. One of the major findings showed that people who had depressive symptoms in their twenties, thirties, or forties were more likely to experience the loss of some memory function. If you are concerned about developing dementia or Alzheimer's, you will understand why this is important to know.

Increased inflammation brings about the risk of hypertension. This increases your risk of having an aneurysm or a stroke. Studies show that people with serious depression are 50 percent more likely to have high blood pressure than people who are not depressed.

The risk of developing arthritis is also increased because of the inflammation in your body. This can be crippling and painful.

Depression makes the diagnosing and treating of cancer more difficult. Drugs and medications will react differently according to your state of mind. Your body reacts better if it can be more joyful.

These are just a few of the way's depression hurts you. If you are experiencing any of these things, start listening to what your body is trying to tell you. It may be one more sign that your soul is on life support.

There are times when life is just overwhelming. Nothing big has to happen. The simplest of things can tip the cart, so to speak. Suddenly, you just feel overwhelmed. Everything seems to be in chaos. All your fears and doubts may come flooding over you. You may try to bury your head in the sand or gaze around in an almost panic. Take a deep breath and know that you are not alone.

In Matthew 6:34 we are taught to "take no thought for the morrow." Basically, no matter what you do, tomorrow is going to take care of itself. This helps to remind us that we are not alone. The Lord is in charge. Psalms 46:1 tells us "God is our refuge and strength, a very present help in trouble." This I am going to promise you. Nothing is going to happen that you cannot get through with God's help.

This is one of those times that it is okay to not be okay. Focus on you right now. What is that still, small voice inside you trying to say? Take time to learn to listen and heed that still, small voice. It may become a matter of life and death.

When you step back and take a breath and rest, it allows the situation to evolve into something that you can heal and grow from. You will become stronger and wiser. You may even be on an entirely different level than before.

Start believing in yourself and trust the process of what is happening. You will be able to come through this and come out stronger. You are here on this earth because you have a purpose. Just as the blade of a sword is repeatedly put into the blacksmith's fire, withdrawn and hammered to temper it and make it stronger, you will always have struggles. Think of it as being tempered into something stronger and finer than you were. Nothing will come your way that you cannot handle with the help of the Lord. He is there for you all the time. All you have to do is sincerely ask. The trials you are going through will come to an end. That deep-down exhaustion will be gone. Just take it one day at a time. Things will change because life is ever evolving.

"He that is slow to anger is better than the mighty..."

Proverbs 16:32

Chapter V

Anger

HYPERSENSITIVITY IS A TERM YOU may hear in various areas. Someone may be hypersensitive to some fragrances such as soaps or cleaners, for instance. Foods may set someone else off. Different medications can be another problem. These can all lead to bigger problems if unattended, but they are not the type of hypersensitivity I am talking about. The question is, "Are you hypersensitive about just about everything?"

When morning comes, do you wake up with a big stretch and a smile on your face? Are you grateful for another day and the challenges and blessings that it will bring? That would be nice, but too often the truth is that you wake up ready to tear into someone. The cat stomps too loudly. You can't find your robe or slippers. The paper is late. You spill coffee on your fresh outfit. You may be tempted to go back to bed and start over. None of it is your fault. How could it be? The world is just out to get you, or so it seems.

Ever find yourself chatting with someone close and they say one thing that triggers such a torrent of anger and frustration that when it is over, you cannot believe what just came out of your mouth? So much anger and resentment poured out that you feel shaken, maybe even ill. What is happening to you?

This is best described as anger. You may ask, where did it come from? You are known for being levelheaded, calm and nice. Over the years, you have found that life has thrown those curve balls we mentioned. You have just sucked it up and kept going. Every disappointment and slight has been buried deep. Your soul has been bombarded again and again.

A deep feeling of bitterness has taken hold. That bitterness manifests itself as anger. Anyone or anything close may become the target of the bitterness and anger that pours forth.

You resent being where you are in life. It is not what you planned or where you saw yourself. That resentment builds into anger and bitterness. Take a look at the classic story by Dickens called *A Christmas Carol*. The main character, Ebenezer Scrooge, is known as a bitter, resentful, and angry man. No one even wants to be around him. The story progresses, and Ebenezer is taken back to several instances from his past. In each of these instances, you can see where his soul was deeply wounded. Each time he became more calloused and bitter. Those deep wounds to the soul were allowed to fester and swell within him to the point that major changes had to be made or he would soon die from it all—lonely, bitter, resentful and angry. Unloved by no other human on earth. Not a very pretty picture.

I used the above story as an example. I am sure that you have met or seen people like that. You may even have been accused of being like that. Things happen that can breed anger deep within us.

Sometimes anger can be good. When it is addressed quickly or expressed in a healthy way, it may even help you think more clearly. This is a healthy benefit. What you need to be concerned about is when it becomes almost all consuming.

Let's take a look at the negative effects anger has on you.

When you hold on to anger or direct it inside, some very negative things happen. There is an old saying that anger turned inward is depression. We just covered the effects of that.

Sometimes you may just explode all over everyone. Doing that not only damages relationships, but it can wreak havoc in your body. Those violent outbursts can physically damage your whole cardiac system. Within the two hours following such an outburst, your chance of having a heart attack doubles. After the outburst, you may feel sick all over or just numb. Both your soul and your body are trying to tell you something. Pay attention to the message.

Repressed anger is not any better. You turn to the use of sarcasm to express the anger indirectly. You find yourself going to great lengths to control it or to just stuff it down inside. There it eats away at you from the inside, causing heart disease as well as some other health issues. Studies show that repressed anger can put you at twice the risk of coronary disease than your cooler-headed colleagues.

Do you know someone who is always red in the face and lashing out at anything and everyone most of the time? Studies show that people like that are three times as prone to suffering a stroke from a blood clot or bleeding within the brain during two hours after one of those angry episodes. If the person has an aneurysm in one of the brain's arteries, the risk becomes six times higher of that aneurysm rupturing.

Anger literally can make you ill. Some studies have shown that just one minute of anger weakens the immune system for the next four to five hours. Research done at Harvard University found that by asking healthy subjects to just remember an incident that really made them angry, caused a significant six-hour dip in their levels of the antibody immunoglobulin A. This is the cell's first line of defense against infection. Ask yourself if it is really worth carrying all that anger around inside.

Strangely, at least in my opinion, anger hurts your lungs even if you are not a smoker. A study done by a group of Harvard scientists on 670 men over an eight-year period, found that the men with the highest hostility or anger ratings had the most decreased lung capacity. This significantly increased their risk of respiratory problems.

When looking at all of this, it is not surprising to learn that anger, undealt with, not only diminishes the quality of life but can significantly shorten it.

It is important to learn to address anger in appropriate ways, instead of burying it until you explode. Learning to express it in constructive ways can actually be very healthy.

There are several scriptures that may be of benefit to you as you make the decision to curb your anger and take a different look at the things in your life.

Psalm 37:8 tells us "Cease from anger and forsake wrath." And Proverbs 14:17 says "He that is soon angry dealeth foolishly." These teach us that even back in ancient times the danger of anger was recognized, when it says that one who is soon to anger usually makes some foolish decision or act. Be honest and think if this has happened to you and put you in an even worse situation than you were originally in.

Proverbs 15:1 instructs us that" A soft answer turneth away wrath; but grievous words stir up anger." Instead of lashing out, take a minute to think about what you really want to express. Catch people off guard by answering softly without malice. See how much better you will feel. You can smile at the surprised looks on their faces.

"Fear thou not; for I am with thee:
be not dismayed; for I am thy
God: I will strengthen thee, yea,
I will uphold thee with the right
hand of my righteousness."

Isaiah 41:10

Chapter VI

Fear

I HAVE SAVED THIS SOUL damager for last. When I first started researching this subject of the wounded soul, this one hit me hard and stirred up all sorts of memories and emotions. In trying to deal with all of them, it became exceedingly difficult to function. Sometimes they were so overwhelming that I could not even write. Wonderful, when one is working with a deadline. What is this mind numbing, soul crippling find, you may ask?

Quite simple. It is plain old fear. A real four-letter word if you will. Fear can eat at you and erode the very soul. It destroys your self-confidence. Fear eats away from any happiness you may find. It makes you feel that your happiness will be snatched away at any minute, just like everything else has been. You find yourself going around waiting for the proverbial shoe to fall or the next blow to catch you. Fear keeps you from reaching out for what you genuinely want or what your real purpose is. You remain silent, instead of speaking up. You do not dare take the chance of failing or being laughed at.

Things happen and life goes on, or so you may think. You have been strong and buried all those fears and gotten on with your life. How has that worked for you?

Have you often felt that something was holding you back?

Have you talked yourself out of doing or trying something because of that deeply buried fear inside you?

Have you allowed yourself to be talked into doing things that you know are wrong for you, just because you are desperate to fit in, to be liked and maybe even loved?

Have you found yourself reading a book or listening to a song lyric or phrase and suddenly all these emotions and memories come rushing to the surface? You are overwhelmed and cannot stop crying. You may be shaking, and you may feel like everything around you is spinning. There are flashes of different times and occurrences—things you do not want to remember or go through again. Why are they coming back to torment you now? It hurts so much, just like when they first happened. Maybe, for a survival technique, you are able to look at them as if they happened to someone else, but deep down you recognize that they happened to you.

This is fear. It may have been buried for decades. You may feel that you were born into an atmosphere of fear and do not know any better. You were taught to fear almost everything. You do not dare step out of the norm.

When some of these things happened, you were an entirely different person than you are now. I am sure that you have grown and changed through the years, but the fear is still there, buried deep in your soul, keeping it from healing.

You probably know of some individuals who do everything for the ones they love, smothering those loved ones and enabling them to avoid growing up and taking responsibility for themselves. These individuals do not realize the harm they are doing in the name of love. They are so afraid of not being loved or needed. If they keep on doing everything for their loved ones maybe they will be loved in return. What they do not realize is if something happened to them tomorrow, their loved ones would continue on and just find another enabler.

Life, at its best, can be very uncertain. On that, we can be in total agreement. Do you allow your mind to roam to those little places that bring all the worst scenarios to the forefront? Do you find yourself obsessing about all the things that could go wrong, instead of enjoying the moment you are in? Do you realize how much joy you have talked yourself out of?

While you have been obsessing about all the negative things that could happen, you have been really damaging your soul with all the negative self-talk and doubt. All the negative feelings and stress build up within you and can make you physically ill. Your soul is looking for peace and a place to heal, but all it is finding is anxiety and confusion.

There is an old story told:

Once there was a man sitting on the side of the road. He looked up and saw Death walking by.

"Hello. What are you going to do today?" he asked.

Death replied, "I am going into the city today, to claim three thousand lives." He proceeded on his way.

That evening, the man was again sitting by the road, when he saw Death coming back from the city.

"You did not tell me the truth. You said you were going to take three thousand lives today, and instead you took ten thousand. How come?"

Death stopped and looked at the man. "I did not lie. I only took the three thousand. Fear took the rest."

In Matthew 6:34, we are taught to "take no thought for tomorrow" because basically, tomorrow will take care of itself. Learn to relax and enjoy the moment. I know that is easier said than done, but please, really try. You may like finding yourself with a little time to be free of worry.

One of my favorite acronyms using the letters in fear is:

False
Evidence
Appearing
Real

Many, but not all, fears are built on misconception. You do not have the whole story.

My husband was named after his father, George. He was referred to as George and his father as Dad. This is how it was in their home.

When my husband was a small child, his parents had another baby. The baby was born at home without a good midwife or doctor. The cord was wrapped too tightly around its neck and the baby was stillborn. Neither George's grandmother nor his father could do anything to help. Instead of blaming her mother, who proclaimed to be a midwife, George's mother blamed her husband.

This tragedy changed the entire atmosphere of my in-law's relationship and the home. It was no longer a happy place. Not being able to accept any guilt herself, or blame her mother, my mother-in-law turned all her anger toward my father-in-law. Not understanding that it was his father who was being talked about, my husband grew up hearing "George killed the baby." This instilled a deep fear in him. He has lived with this fear, that he will do something that will ruin any happiness that he has found. A misconception? Yes. You can see that he did not have the entire story and all he knew was that everyone was angry or sad and "George" was to blame.

Right or wrong, little children tend to take the blame if something bad happens in their family. This can become a very real and paralyzing fear.

This is an extreme situation, and I hope that nothing that serious has happened to you. This is not meant to say that the fears you have are not very real to you. They are a result of something that shook you or radically changed your direction in ways you do not know. They have frightened you so much that you are afraid that you will not make it through again. You feel all alone with your fear.

Now is the time to remember, and be assured that if you got through it the first time, you will make it through a second time, and it will be easier. The difference is that instead of shoving that fear deeper within you, you are going to bring it out into the light and see it for what it really is. This time, you have a better understanding of the circumstances. and what happened to make you so afraid. By facing that fear and others, you are able to start to heal.

One of my very favorite scriptures is Isaiah 41:10. It tells us to "fear thou not; for I am with thee: be not dismayed; for I am thy God; I will strengthen thee; yea; I will uphold thee with the right hand of my righteousness." What wonderful comfort that can give you. You are not alone. If you but ask, the Lord will strengthen you and help you. What more do you really need?

Did you grow up the phrase "What will the neighbors think?" One more way of making sure that you are going to be afraid to walk outside the given lines. Afraid to be different in any way. Instead of searching for and then finding your purpose, you have accepted the norm, kept your head down and done what was expected of you. Now you find yourself with feelings of being lost. Circumstances have changed over the years and you find yourself at a juncture where you would very much like to make some changes, but that deeply buried fear is in the way. It is something that needs to be addressed if any positive changes are to be made in your life.

Proverbs 3:25-26 may help. It states, "Be not afraid of sudden fear… For the Lord shall be thy confidence…depend on the Lord." 2 Timothy 1:7 instructs us "For God hath not given us a spirit of fear: but of power. And of love, and of a sound mind."

Do you realize that fear is such a very powerful tool that it is most often used against us? When you look at different people down through the ages of time, you will see where civilizations were held captive time and again by rulers and despots controlling them by means of fear. Unfortunately, there are many areas in the world that are still ruled that way today.

"Terrible," you may say. True, but how often have you allowed yourself to be controlled by fear? Preposterous! Not really. When was the last time you did something because if you didn't, you might lose your job or not get the position in the first place? Have you ever felt pressured into something because someone may withhold their love from you if you do not comply? Be honest. Have you ever used fear to control a child or pet? Have you ever told your child that they would be punished or not get an anticipated treat if they did not behave? Have you raised your voice to get their attention and acted very scary? Did the child or dog cower in front of you? Using fear can be very effective, but is it really the best way to teach or lead?

Gandhi once said:
>"The enemy is fear.
>We think it is hate, but it is fear."

How many times have you spoken against or struck out at something or someone with anger simply because it was foreign to you? You were like the cornered animal that snarls and growls and strikes out. This is not because the animal hates you. It is because it is in a situation that is unknown, and it is afraid. That fear can cause its destruction, not hate, but fear. Perhaps it is time for you to learn to take the time to act instead of reacting to something.

Recognizing and letting go of that fear helps you and your soul to begin some serious healing.

"Our faith in Jesus Christ enables
us to meet any challenge."
Carole M. Stephens

Chapter VII

Conclusion

WE HAVE COVERED A LOT of material in a short time. I hope that some of it has opened your eyes to a few of the underlying causes of your present situation. Your spirit is in serious need of being revived. In this case, shock paddles and a defibrillator are not the answer.

Every person is different. There is no one, fast and sure solution that fits all people and all things. In the second section of this book, we will go over different scenarios and offer suggestions for helping to revive your spirit. Remember that nothing works if you do not work at and with it.

Before we begin that section there are some truths for you to digest and get a handle on.

The first is that God is the father of our spirit. Our spirits are nurtured and strengthened by eternal truth and prayer.

The second is that God is the same yesterday, today and tomorrow. He does not change. We, however, do change, and not always for the best. There is an old saying about not feeling as close to God as we once did. If that is the case, may I ask, "Who moved?" Whenever you travel do you take time to frequently check the route you are on? Why? Because you do not want to stray too far off course and get lost, correct? What if you checked how your walk with the Lord is going as often as you check your other routes? Each day, we must seek the Lord in both scripture and prayer, to find out how we are doing and to grow closer to Him.

It is often said," To the victor go the spoils." In this third point we start to realize that it is really the one who endures to the end who receives the prize. You were not brought into this world to just float along with the current of life. Instead you came with the power to think, and reason, and most importantly, achieve. You were not sent here with a spirit of failure but with a spirit to succeed gloriously. Do not let anyone, including yourself, try to make you believe differently.

Fourth is to not get discouraged and quit. As long as you have breath in your body, it is not too late. Both Mary Kay Ash and Henry Ford have been attributed with having said, "If you think you can, you can. If you think you can't, you can't."

If you never attempt to do something, you will not achieve anything. Are you afraid of failing? Do you let that hold you back from a life not lived fully? Albert Einstein said, "Anyone who has never failed, has never tried anything new." Henry Ford encouraged with this message, "Failure is simply the opportunity to begin again, this time more intelligently." Remember that Edison had ten thousand failures before his success with the light bulb.

Step back and take a long look around you. Are you really in the present or are you trying to avoid it? Consider the present with great fortitude. Now look toward the future with confidence. Always remember that you cannot change the past, but you are able to shape the future.

Healing from the damage of the past does not mean that you forget the damage ever happened. It means that the damage no longer controls who you are. Healing brings strength and peace and most of all courage.

You have been given a chance to heal, grow and find that harmony and purpose for your life. You are a very precious child of God and do deserve it.

Are you ready to begin your journey of healing and reviving your spirit? I promise it will be worth it and you will be strengthened and revitalized.

"For whoso findeth me findeth life,
and shall obtain favor of the Lord."

Proverbs 8:35

Part II

Chapter VIII

CPR for the Wounded Soul

A LOT OF PEOPLE ACCUSE me of being too direct and cut and dried. Perhaps I am, but when a solution is in sight, I have the tendency to zero in and focus on the main goal. In this case, it is helping the soul to heal.

In reading this book, you have identified the problem. Your soul is so very wounded and tired and in need of some real care, rest and love. It is already beginning to heal because you now recognize the situation. What more can you do to promote healing? How do you prevent it from happening again?

The first, and what I identify as the most important thing you can do, is to start loving yourself. Yes, you read that correctly. Start loving yourself. I am not telling you to become narcissistic but start giving yourself a break. Like most people, you probably cannot just take an unlimited amount of time to get away somewhere and lay back and heal. You still have to go out into the battlefield each day. This can be a bit of a dilemma. Hopefully, this will provide tools to help you heal and still continue to function in the everyday world. Know that, in order to heal, you are going to have to learn to do some things differently. They may feel uncomfortable at first, but that will pass as you start to feel the difference.

It has been said that insanity is doing the same thing the same way over and over and expecting a different result. This is why it is important for you to start with some changes no matter how small at first. That first step is loving yourself.

Loving yourself is so particularly important. When you do not really love yourself, it affects your entire life. That includes everything from the dreams that you have to your health. I am not trying to give the impression that I think people are out to get you, but when you do not love yourself, there are people who pick up on that and take advantage of you. We need to fix that.

Psychologists and self-help gurus have promoted learning to love yourself for decades or longer. One of the steps they strongly promote is for you to get really close to a mirror and look eyeball to eyeball at yourself and repeat "I love you" ten times several times a day. The claim is that over time it helps to reprogram certain parts in the brain. I have recommended it myself until I learned better.

We have already established that your soul is on life support. Now imagine standing beside someone laying in a bed, hooked up to all the various life support systems. Several times a day you get close to them and say that you love them. Is that going to bring them out of their coma and heal them? It is not very likely. They may hear you, but more action is needed to revive them.

This is true with your spirit. Telling it that you love yourself is all well and good, but you really need to take a bit more positive action to get the results you are hoping for.

Part of learning to love yourself is taking steps to change some of your routine. Start by unplugging as many of your electrical devices as possible. I understand that you may have a position that requires you to be constantly on call, like a medical person or such. Most of us are not in that type of situation. Unplug as much as possible. Turn off social media for a time. Neither you nor the world will stop. Recently, many of the people in my church were advised to turn off social media or go on a fast from it for a week and then record their feelings. Many reported feeling freer, having more time for family or themselves. Fasting from social media helped me to tune in and hear what my body and soul were trying to tell me. It is very important that we do not allow our daily activities to shut out or hinder communication with our spirit. Try it and see what your results are. You might consider recording them in a journal.

Whether you realize it or not, your brain and soul thrive on the quiet. The constant bombardment of information and conversation harms your mood, performance and health. You need the downtime to draw inward. Let your mind just wander and daydream. When was the last time you did that?

A recent survey by the Bureau of Labor Statistics found that about 83 percent of the people claim that they spend no time during the day relaxing or just thinking. They consistently overwork and overdo. Basically, they treat themselves like machines. This is especially true of women who feel that the best way to succeed is to do as many productive tasks as possible. Are you identifying with any of this? Are you exhausted, and have a zombie-like feeling that happens when you have just finished what seems like a gazillion meetings, or an insane day filled with errands and chores? Do you start Monday feeling like you just finished a half marathon, because your weekend was filled with too many events and gatherings? You find yourself being forgetful, under productive, and very drained. Going at life full bore is not the way to be your most creative and productive or happy and content.

Your mind, body and spirit need time off—some down time to recuperate. You may believe that it is not possible to take any time like that, that it is a waste of productive time. Research shows that when you take a little mental down time several times during the day, you actually become more focused and energized. This down time is time spent letting your mind daydream and wander. This allows you to come up with new ideas, become more creative and find solutions.

You were created with the design to have regular rest periods. You have two main modes of processing things. The first is the action mode. This is where you work, interact, watch tv, scroll through email and Instagram, and make sense of all the information that is coming at you.

The second is the default mode network (DMN). It comes on whenever your brain takes a break from everything. Example: How many times have you been reading something and then realized that you have no idea what you read or where you may be? You were probably thinking about something totally unrelated like what to have for supper. Research shows that the DMN can switch on and off in a matter of moments. I am sure that you have found yourself zoning out from time to time, sometimes for longer than you may realize. It may feel similar to when you are sitting and watching the waves wash in and out at the beach.

It is very important that you do not ignore this. Spending time in the DMN is crucial to your wellbeing. It helps you clarify who you are, and what you need to do next. The meaning of life. It rejuvenates you and helps you to heal. It helps to clarify what lessons you have learned, to dream and plan for the future, and to work out problems. Hopefully, you can see where taking a break several times a day can prevent that drained feeling and help you to concentrate.

You understand why turning off all news programs after seven in the evening is important. Listening to the stories on these programs, when you are supposed to be unwinding, brings on more stress. You either worry about things you can do little to nothing about or you let fear creep in from all the horrible things out there. Some of the things you hear might stir up feelings of intense anger that only hurts you or the ones around you. Is it worth it?

Cease to be tied to your phone. As you scroll through it just for something to do, you are robbing yourself of some of the precious down-time, healing time.

When I go out to meet friends or shop, I stow it in my purse. That way it is there in an emergency, but it is not in charge. Try it and see if you feel freer and less distracted. You now have time to appreciate your surroundings and to let your mind wander among the possibilities. When you unplug like that, it allows you to hear that still small voice. It allows your spirit to connect with the Spirit. Learn to hear and heed that still, small voice. Become familiar with it. This is really a matter of life and death.

On the subject of unplugging, let's take it one step further. Schedule a mini vacation for yourself. If time and circumstances won't allow a real trip, then make it a staycation. The important thing is to be unplugged. At first you may experience some anxiety or guilt about taking time for yourself, but that will pass. Stop worrying about what you may be missing out on in the media, and tune into what you have been denying yourself. Take a long soak in the tub. Listen to soothing music. Read a good book or some scriptures. Do something that you used to enjoy or have always wanted to try but have never taken the time for. Let yourself relax and let go. When you return from your mini vacation, work at being a little less connected. Your mind and body will appreciate it.

Stop comparing yourself to other people. Learn to love yourself. You are a unique individual sent here to fulfill a spot that no one else can. I understand that it can be very tempting to drool over your friend's new car or some celebrity's tropical vacation. Do you realize that every minute you spend comparing your life to someone else's is sixty seconds that you are not focusing on your own dreams or goals?

It is extremely easy to be hard on ourselves. We are so overextended in all that we do, it is easier to look at all that we did not get done, rather than what we have accomplished. Starting a type of gratitude journal or a daily list of each achievement can help. Write it just before bed. It helps you sleep better. Instead of fretting about what got missed, enjoy what got done.

Once a friend gave me a book to use as a gratitude journal, when once again I was moving to another area. As I look back on this difficult time, I can testify that writing down accomplishments and things I was grateful for each day strengthened me and soothed a sometimes-aching heart.

It does not have to be pages of things. Start with just writing down five things that you accomplished or that made you feel good that day. It changes your perspective. It allows you to be a little easier on yourself.

Learn to say "no" sometimes. We all have our limits and need to acknowledge them. It is alright to be human. Remember that you are not a machine, but a special human being.

I once had a very dear friend named Barb. Barb thought she had to help everyone. Barb held a part-time job at a doctor's office. She would rush over to the nearby daycare center on break to nurse her baby. Barb helped her husband run his own business. In her spare time, Barb was typing a manuscript for another friend. Barb could never say "no" to anyone. When she started to slip and not be able to meet all the demands on herself, she was hospitalized, medicated, and sent back out into her world. No directions were given about slowing down or changing her routine. This became a recurring cycle over the next few months. One day, when her child was a little past his second birthday, Barb put a gun to her head and pulled the trigger. She was so exhausted, and her spirit was so wounded that she chose not to go on.

The next time someone asks you to do something that you just do not have the time or energy and desire to add to your already busy schedule, you might tell them, "Thanks for thinking of me, but I just do not have the time that the project deserves." Most people will understand that and not hold it against you.

Stop being so critical of yourself. When things are not going well, you probably have the tendency to beat yourself up and not like yourself very much. Why? Are you really upset with how inept you feel, or are you afraid that if you are not perfect in every way, you will not be accepted or loved? Being a perfectionist puts so much added stress on you and takes so much extra time. You want it all to be so exact that the project never gets done or even started. This can actually harm and hinder your performance in both your personal and professional life. The exact opposite effect you are hoping for.

No matter how they may look on the outside, no one is perfect. We all hide behind our masks and put up a front for others to see. Remember, there has only been one perfect person who ever lived and walked the earth and that was Jesus Christ, the son of God.

To make a positive change, accept that you are an imperfect person sent into an imperfect world to learn perfection. The key word being learn. Too often you may forget that you are a special child of a loving Heavenly Father. This is an old question, but a good one: "If God loves you, who are you not to?"

The world likes to tell you that you do not measure up in so many ways. THE WORLD LIES. You are unique—one of a kind. You were sent here for a purpose. Your assignment is to find out what that purpose is and to follow through. When you are able to do that, the changes you are seeking will follow.

I came across this anonymous poem on Facebook that seems to say it all.

The Other Serenity Prayer

God grant me the serenity to stop beating myself up,
for not doing things perfectly.
The courage to forgive myself,
Because I am working on doing better,
And the wisdom to know that You already love
Me just the way I am.

"Set thine house in order... ."

2 Kings 20:1

Chapter IX

Drowning in Too Much Stuff

ARE YOU DROWNING IN TOO Much Stuff?

In an article that I recently read, it was stated that the average person has up to three hundred thousand things. That seems like a bit of an exaggeration, but even half that amount is too much in my opinion. I probably developed this opinion because of my husband's late aunt. She was a very dear person, but she was a major hoarder. You literally walked through aisles of containers that were stacked above your head to get from one room to another. She had four chest freezers that were packed full of food. Most of the food was way outdated. All of that stuff controlled her life. She was afraid to throw anything out or give it away because it might be needed someday. After her passing, it took five dumpsters to hold all the stuff she had been saving. Either no one wanted it, or it was not worth saving. It had, unfortunately, controlled her life and held her captive.

Look around at your surroundings. Are they cluttered with things you no longer use or that do not give you pleasure anymore? Are you starting to drown in too much stuff? Why are you saving all of it? Do you honestly believe that cute dress or pair of pants crammed in your already too full closet is magically going to fit you again someday?

You are not meant to hang onto all of that. Scriptures give you example after example of the Lord providing for your needs. Many of his missionaries were sent out with only the clothes on their backs. He provided shelter and food all along the way for them. He will provide your needs as well.

Do you know how many wild monkeys are caught? A box is set in an open area. Inside the box is a piece of fruit. On the side of the box is a small hole just big enough for the monkey's front paw to go through. The monkey puts his paw through the hole and finds the fruit. He then tries to pull it out of the box. His paw with the fruit in it, is too big to fit back through the hole. Rather than let go of the fruit, the monkey will sit and allow itself to be captured. My point is, "How much of you is being held captive by all the unnecessary stuff or clutter?"

Clutter seems to be the accepted word right now. Whatever you want to call it, stuff, belongings, clutter, etc. It all has the same result. It is harmful to your well-being and to your soul. You are drowning.

Studies have shown that clutter harms both your physical and mental health. Physically, the dust from all that clutter can bring about respiratory problems, not to mention the extra energy you must expend to try to clean it all. Sometimes you may find that your soul just does not have the energy to deal with it. It drags you down to the point that you can't cope with much of anything.

Clutter increases your stress levels. People living with constant clutter are shown to have more depression, are more fatigued, and have higher levels of cortisol in their systems. The cortisol levels fail to decline during the day, and this can lead to chronic stress, disease and even a higher mortality risk. High cortisol levels also may be responsible for increased weight, especially around the middle. If this describes your home, it is not a restful haven to regroup and heal in.

When a person is in a prolonged stressful environment, they often seek or come up with coping mechanisms. They may just sit and try to block out everything around them. They may binge watch something on television. Often, they will grab some good old comfort food and totally indulge themselves. In other words, clutter helps you blow your diet among other things.

When you are surrounded by clutter, unfinished projects and piles of things, you may feel anxious, unsatisfied, and sometimes want to beat yourself up, so you revert back to unhealthy habits to cope and make you feel better.

Clutter can threaten the safety of you and your family. Many of the items may be flammable. How many doors and windows are partially or totally blocked? How would you and your loved ones get out in case of emergency?

Clutter may upset your children. I know that can be hard to believe when you look in some of their rooms. If your home itself is badly cluttered, not only you but your children may be uncomfortable inviting anyone over. Studies show that the children may be less happy and have a harder time making friends when they come from cluttered homes.

Excessive clutter can have a negative influence on your love life. If you are single, the clutter may make you hesitant to invite anyone over, especially a potential suitor. If you are in a long-term serious relationship, clutter may cause you to overlook subtle changes that need to be made to strengthen that relationship. Excessive clutter may lead to a higher chance of divorce.

Clutter can affect your employment and hurt your chances for advancement. Frequent absences and a messy desk do not give good vibes to your employer. Messy desks can cut back on your productivity because the clutter distracts you from the task as it competes for your attention.

Clutter has a way of damaging your finances in more than the aforementioned way. People who live with excessive clutter tend to purchase things on impulse without any agenda. Many times, it is an item that they already have. Paying bills can be a challenge when you can't find them.

You can see and understand where this adds more strain on an already overburdened soul.

One of the lessons that is important for all of us to learn is to let go. The scriptures promise that the Lord is there for you in all things. He will help you and provide a way for you to obtain all that you need. You and your soul can rest assured of that.

Just as you need to trust and learn to let go of the clutter in your surroundings, you need to let go of the clutter in your mind. That situation or problem that you are trying so hard to solve can be very draining. You pray about it, and nothing seems to happen. It may even appear to become worse.

- May I ask you, have you truly turned it over to the Lord, or are you hanging onto one little corner of it or trying to direct the Lord in the final outcome? In case you have not figured it out, turning things over to the Lord does not work that way. You have to let go of ALL of it and trust that He knows what is best for all concerned. No, the way things may turn out is not always the way you wanted or thought they should, but when you look back, you will see that it was the best way for all concerned.

It is important to understand that only by letting go, clearing out the old and unused, can there be room for the new healing and growth. Just as a surgeon cuts out a bad growth from your body, you need to rid yourself of what is harming you. This includes your physical surroundings and your mental and spiritual situations.

How do you go about this? How do you know what to do first? Start where you are, even before you may feel ready. God never sends you more than you are ready for with His help. You are not alone in this.

Start in one small area. Clean off your dresser or a small table. Make it sparkle. See how looking at it makes you feel. If it all seems overwhelming, invite a friend over that you can trust to be a little on the ruthless side when it comes to getting rid of unnecessary items. Make a couple of piles—things to donate, things to pitch, things to sell, things to keep.

The basic rules to go by are:

- Have you used it in the last two years?
- Does it give you pleasure?
- If the answer is no to either of these questions, let it go.

Take pictures of some of the mementos and then donate the item. Some items, you may worry that you might need. Ask yourself if it is an item you could borrow or rent. Value the space that is being taken up rather than the item itself.

Find ways to organize the items you keep. Put up hooks for hanging coats and purses. Baskets or little trays are handy for small items like keys.

Set up automatic payments for as many of your bills as possible. Use an envelope system for the others. Have an envelope for each of them and the date clearly marked on the outside as to when each is due. Either put cash or a check in the envelope so the money is there when the payment is due. Some people use a notebook with the scheduled monthly payments written in neat columns for easy reading. Put the notebook beside the calendar on your desk or work area. Take a few minutes each week to sort papers into the keep pile and the circular file to pitch.

The scriptures teach us that we are to make our homes clean and orderly like a holy place. This becomes a place for you to come to and regroup from the world. A soothing place for your troubled soul to feel at ease and heal. Each of us needs a sanctuary where we can feel safe. This is something that your soul is asking for.

In having a neat and orderly place to live, a lot of your depression may start to lift. You may look at a finished area and burst into tears for seemingly no reason. They may be tears of joy and happiness. They can be tears that release so many emotions, you don't know what to do. To add to all of this emotion, you can't stop the tears. That is okay. Tears help to cleanse the soul. Any number of emotions may come up, and the tears cleanse and make them better.

Sometimes, not always, depression comes from all sorts of pent-up emotions you have never taken time to acknowledge. Cleansing unnecessary things from your physical surroundings can be metaphoric to cleansing things from your soul. Remember, it is only by cleaning out the old that we have room for the new and wonderful blessings and gifts that Heavenly Father has for us.

"And the second is like, namely this, Thou shalt love thy neighbor as thyself ....."

Mark 12:31

Chapter X

Forgiving

"AS I HAVE LOVED YOU, love one another."

These words of a favorite hymn have been going through my mind. Sometimes they feel like something is sitting on my shoulder urging me to share this and its importance. It is actually the second great commandment given to us from Jesus Christ during his ministry here on earth. Sometimes it is referred to as the Golden Rule. Actually, it is the first half of that rule. We will cover the second half later on.

Simply stated, because God first and always loves us, unconditionally, we are to love and forgive others. How can you deny others what you so freely have been given?

Are you a person who holds grudges against others? Do you nurture those hurts that you feel came from them? Now take a look at those you are nursing these grudges against. Is it hurting them at all? Are they continuing with their lives like nothing has happened? Maybe to them, nothing did happen. Could it be that someone does not have all of the story?

Be honest now, who are these grudges hurting the most? Look in the mirror. You will find your answer there.

I once knew a very pretty young woman. At least she was pretty on the outside. We will call her Jane for now. Jane liked to be noticed and was jealous of anyone who seemed to get more attention than she did. She started holding grudges and plotting revenge for all of the slights she felt. A great bitterness grew inside her, being constantly fed by her unforgiving nature. Gradually, as that bitterness could no longer be contained on the inside, it began to show on her face and in her health. Ultimately, who did Jane do the most harm to?

It takes large amounts of energy to hold and nurture grudges. Do you have the extra energy to devote to doing that? Your spirit does not need all the energy draining dark thoughts that are associated with that grudge. Let go and forgive. Your spirit will thank you.

Are you someone who is drawn to gossip? We, as humans, have a tendency to be very curious. Gossip can have a strong pull. Maybe you are drawn to listening to it, to make yourself feel better. So and so is not that perfect after all.

Do you hear a story about someone and then embellish it as you pass it on? You know deep down that what you are saying is not true, but it feels good to have the spotlight for a few seconds.

Sometimes gossip is used as a means to get even for some wrong, real or imagined. Is revenge worth possibly damaging someone else's life? Will it heal you and make you whole? Maybe you grew up hearing about getting even or striking back at someone. In Deuteronomy 32:35 the Lord teaches "To me belongeth vengeance…" This means that He knows more than you and that all things will be made right in His time.

Listening to and spreading gossip is really demeaning to you. You are worth so much more. There is an old saying," If you cannot say something nice about someone, do not say anything at all." When you hold yourself apart from such things, eventually people will know and recognize your good character. When you do say something, it will be listened to. Before you speak, ask yourself the following things: Is it true? Is it uplifting? Is it worthy to be said?

When you learn to love yourself, you do not have to put people down to lift yourself up. You do not have to elevate yourself by pointing out others real or made up flaws and mistakes.

Now that we have discussed the harm you do to yourself when you gossip about others, let's look at what you do to yourself with all that negative self- talk. Each time you put yourself down, your poor spirit takes another hit. This is not to say that you should not recognize and admit when you make mistakes. Mistakes happen. Admit it and grow from them.

When the mistakes or setbacks do occur, take the time to allow yourself to feel. Instead of stuffing it down like you have before, let yourself experience the feeling. you are having. Put a name to each of them—embarrassment, guilt, anger, disappointment, all of them. This helps your soul to catch its breath and let you put things into perspective.

This is probably not your first mistake or setback. If it is, you have not tried very much. Think back to when you have gone through something similar. What skills did you use to get through them? What strengths and coping skills did you acquire? Smile at how resilient you were. Use those memories now to find the resilience that is needed to pull yourself up. Congratulate yourself that you even tried. Take a look at the experience and see what you have learned from it. This will help you determine which direction to go in now and what skills you need to sharpen.

Now that you have achieved some perspective, let's take a look at what happened. Did you attempt something new? Did it have a very steep learning curve? Did you set your standards too high? Instead of being so hard on yourself, try strategizing about what you are going to do next. It is only a failure if you allow it to stop you. These mistakes and setbacks help us to appreciate our successes more.

Instead of retreating and licking your wounds, reach out to a friend or family member for help or just someone to talk to. When you share, you may find yourself actually laughing about part of what happened. This helps to lighten your mood and reframe your difficulties. Learn how others may have gotten through similar trials. This resilience helps you become more optimistic and stronger.

Life is full of many obstacles. The old "two steps forward, one step back" should actually be two steps forward, three steps around an obstacle, and one step back. Learning to plan and anticipate some of the obstacles helps to avoid some of the setbacks and gives you a bit more self-confidence.

Simply put, stop talking down to yourself and getting discouraged. Focus on what you have learned and move ahead with a plan. With the help of the Lord, you can accomplish what you set out to do. Identify your purpose and work toward fulfilling it.

We talked briefly about how you are treating other people. Putting others down to build yourself up is never the way to go. One should never look down upon another person unless you are helping them up.

Each of us has been sent here for a different reason or purpose. You are having a hard-enough time identifying your own purpose, without criticizing another who may be just as lost in their own way.

Remember that you have been taught to love one another, like Christ has loved you.

"He that loveth not knoweth
not God; for God is love."

1 John 4:8

Chapter XI

Loving Yourself

"LOVE OTHERS AS YOU LOVE yourself," or, "Do unto others as you would do unto yourself." These are platitudes that you have probably heard time and again. They hold valuable truths.

I have said that loving others was only the first part of the second great commandment. We have a habit of skipping over or not listening to the second part. It speaks of self-love and how we treat ourselves. If you are not loving and taking care of yourself, how do you have anything to give to others? Without loving yourself, the well runs dry and your poor spirit becomes starved.

How do you go about loving yourself and not appearing self-centered or rude? Take stock of what you really enjoy doing. Are there things that you want to try or to get back to having in your life? What things used to give you pleasure before you got too busy for them?

You may claim that you do not have the energy or time for such things, and that is why you are not doing them. You do know that excuse is one of the reasons you are where you are at right now. If you choose for things to be different, then you have to start doing some things differently. It does not have to be some huge giant step, just a few baby steps forward will help more healing to begin.

Set some goals for yourself. Now look at them and ask yourself if they are big goals or are, they readily attainable? Sometimes you may set goals that are wonderful, but how do you go about attaining them? The same way you eat an elephant, one bite at a time. Look at what you are aiming for and break it down into steps that you are able to manage. Say that you would like to create a fabulous painting. First, you might look around to see if there are some art classes being offered near you and sign up for one. There you will learn what materials and tools you are going to need. Try working in different mediums, to see which feels right for you. Ask questions. Read books on the subject. Develop the technique that feels comfortable. Each of these is a step toward your goal. Enjoy each step along the way. When you are ready, you will be able to put down on canvas what you feel inside. You will have achieved your goal. Your spirit will feel so good.

When you are complimented, do you find yourself trying to place some of the credit on another person? Do you mentally scramble to find a way to compliment them right back? It is okay to claim your success. Just learn to smile and say, "thank you." That is all that is needed.

It is wonderful to pat yourself on the back for each of your achievements along the way. At first you may be afraid of appearing arrogant or overly ambitious as you move forward in making positive changes. That is okay.

As you are taking steps to complete your goal, you may find that there are some other goals or changes you want to make. If you decide on a complete career change or a change in how you relate to the Lord, that is fine. As you go through different phases in your life, it is perfectly okay to reinvent yourself. Remember that we talked about finding your purpose in life. As you and your life both change, those purposes can and will change as well. Don't be afraid of them. Embrace them. They are part of the journey.

Build a firm belief in yourself. Do not let others put you down. Perhaps they are afraid of the change in you because they cannot face the idea of changing themselves. When there are changes that you are choosing and feeling good about, you will find that there will be some people you may choose to avoid because they are the ones who continually try to drag you back. Learn to walk away from people who put you down. Stay away from disagreements that will never be resolved. Stop trying to please people who will never see or understand your true worth. Being strong and avoiding those types of people is vital to your healing and growth. The more you walk away from these things that poison your soul, the healthier you will become. As you improve, others will come into your life that you have more in common with or that recognize the special spirit that you are. It is hard to change old habits, but it is essential if you are to grow.

Learn to speak up and speak out. The following is not meant to offend or ignore my male readers. It is just a fact, that we can all learn from. While we women are accused of talking too much, it has been shown that in business and social settings, women do not get as much airtime as men. Each of us needs to learn how important it is to speak up and find your authentic voice. Do not be shy, be informed. You may have an answer that someone else needs.

Speaking out when you see injustice can be very scary and maybe dangerous in today's atmosphere of political correctness. Remember that

when you stand by in silence, when you know that you should protest, that is what cowards are made of. If you do not speak up for others who can't, who will speak up for you when and if that day should come?

"He maketh me to lie down in green pastures; he leadeth me beside the still waters. He restoreth my soul."

Psalm 23:2-3

Chapter XII

Caring for Yourself

GET OUTSIDE WHENEVER POSSIBLE. BREATHE deeply and clear yourself of all those negative feelings. If possible, stroll through the park or the woods. Get away from the traffic sounds and other people. Listen to the sounds of nature like the chirping of birds and the rustling of the leaves on the trees. Enjoy the site of a rabbit scurrying around. Laugh at the antics of a squirrel chattering at you from a tree. Feel the soothing effect of the green space around you. This gives your brain more time to relax and roam around. You never know where those thoughts and ideas may lead.

Several studies have been conducted on the positive effects of walking. Did you know that just three minutes of walking helps your blood pressure to decrease, and five minutes improves your mood? When you get close to ten minutes your creative thinking improves. If you walk for fifteen minutes after a meal, your digestion improves, and your blood sugar levels decrease. Thirty minutes of walking after a meal can help you lose weight. You do have to walk and not just stroll for it to affect your weight. Forty minutes of good walking helps reduce the risk of developing coronary heart disease. Take that up to ninety minutes and the depressive thoughts reduce and lighten. Not quite the runner's high, but easier on your body.

Some of you may be lucky enough to live in areas where you can go barefoot. You may have been lectured about the importance of wearing shoes to protect your feet. While there is some truth to that, the fact of the matter is that you were born without shoes, and your body likes it when you go barefoot. Letting your unshod feet come in contact with the ground provides several healing benefits you may not be aware of.

People talk about being or getting grounded. Come to find out, that is not just something that is talked about. You do not just sit on a chair somewhere and learn to breathe deeply to try to center yourself. The real grounding, no pun intended, is when you go barefoot outside. When your bare feet touch the beautiful natural earth, all sorts of free electrons are transferred through the soles of your feet throughout the entire body. This grounding effect is one of the most potent antioxidants we know of. Wow, and it did not come out of a bottle from the health store. It is free. A gift from the Lord.

Weather permitting, find a spot and learn to enjoy being barefoot in the dirt. Sometimes when I have been incredibly stressed, I like to find a quiet spot and sit on the ground with my bare feet being tickled by the grass. After about fifteen minutes, I feel more myself and ready to face the world again. Try it. You really have nothing to lose and a whole lot to gain from it.

An effective way of getting back to loving yourself and making your spirit happy is to make a list of things that you really love to do. Do you love to read or cook? When was the last time you binged out on your favorite movie or went to a concert with friends? Maybe you like to skate, play tennis or tickle the old ivories on the piano. Think about activities that fulfill and enrich you. They can be very rejuvenating and energizing. You may find yourself feeling more alive than you have in ages.

Playtime or playdates are not just for children. Time to play or have fun is just as vital to adults as well. Make it a priority to carve out a time for enjoyment. Learn to have fun again. It is wonderful to experience all the positive emotions that come from a little bit of play time.

While you make that list of things that you love to do, it may be a good time to recognize and cut out as much of the stuff you hate as possible. It is really important to stop doing the things that you hate. They damage your spirit and they harm you.

There is an old saying about laughter healing the soul. It really does. Laughter relieves tension and makes you look younger. Who doesn't want that? When you smile at others, even complete strangers, they usually smile back. When you laugh, many will join in even when they have no idea what is so funny. It is very contagious so spread it around.

Laughter has been proven to be very strong medicine. Just one minute of laughter raises your immune system for the next twenty-four hours.

Years ago, there was a famous man, Norman Lear, who received a very dire diagnosis from the doctor. Choosing not to accept that prognosis, the man bought all of the funny movies he could think of. He then rented a hotel room. Taking the movies, he retreated to the hotel room and watched the comedies and laughed for the next month. When he emerged from the self-imposed isolation, he went back to his doctor. The doctor could find nothing wrong with him. The month of laughing had cured him. I know that this may sound a bit dramatic, but it proves a point about learning to laugh again.

Encourage the softer side of you to come out. It is alright to be vulnerable. You do not have to be tough and strong and right all the time. Scriptures teach us that the Lord is there and that He will use our weaknesses as strengths. No matter what, keep practicing that positive self-talk.

Is there a challenge or opportunity out there that you have been thinking about? What is stopping you? Are you over thinking it from every angle imaginable? Given a little time you can find any number of reasons to not do something. On the other hand, you may think so long and hard about accepting the challenge or going after that opportunity, that you are too late. It has passed you by. Why are you letting fear and doubt dictate your life?

Whatever challenge is in front of you, like a promotion with more responsibility or a tough talk with a friend or loved one, avoiding it means that you are stuck. When faced with challenges of life or the opportunities that are offered, pray first for direction and strength. Take a deep breath and forge ahead. By facing what is in front of you, small step by small step, you will gain more confidence in yourself. Your spirit will feel lighter and more alive.

Are you a strict rule follower? Like most, maybe you were taught the importance of being polite, doing what is asked when it is asked, and minding your manners. Ever wish you could be different, or have you broken a few of the rules already? Did you know that it is the rule breakers who change the world?

Be creative. Start small if you wish. It does not have to be something on a large scale or grand. It just needs to be satisfying to you. Make your spirit feel good. Do not be afraid to break the rules. I said rules, not law. I don't want you getting arrested or fined for something, after all. We are talking about doing something pleasurable and fun for you. Stop being a perfectionist and just have fun. You have earned it. Own your wonderful uniqueness and never ever compare yourself to anyone else.

"Creative expression can also represent
the celebration of our gratitude to
God for our gifts and talents."
Neal A. Maxwell

Chapter XIII

Healing from Anger

IN THE FIRST SECTION, THE damage that anger can do to you was discussed. It is clearly not an ideal way to live, for you or anyone else.

How do you face this problem before you self-destruct? Let's try to identify where it is coming from, okay? Has it just become a habit over time? Have you forgotten how to be any other way? Is your spirit so tired that striking out seems easier? The following are some suggestions that may help you start a new pattern.

- Learn to act instead of reacting.
- Take a moment to be silent. While you are taking that moment, pray.
- Take a deep breath before you speak.
- Speak quietly and calmly while you address the situation.

Notice how much better you feel. Notice the surprised looks of your companions. Smile.

Another reason for your anger may be a deeply buried fear. Just like an animal will strike out viciously when feeling afraid and helpless, you learned to keep the demons at bay by striking out in much the same way. Please take a moment to consider this. Was there a time that you can remember when you did not feel angry all the time? Was there a time when you felt safe and protected? When did that change? Can you identify what changed? Was it something big and life changing or something small that only you really noticed and felt affected by?

Whatever it was, you have been left with a deep feeling that if you do not strike first, you will lose, or not be of value. Trust me when I say that you will lose more by continuing to strike out than you can imagine. You got through whatever this trauma was the first time. With help from the Lord, you can go back through it in your mind and release it. It may take a little work and more than a little courage to face it again, but until you do, you and your spirit are suffering. It has become a blockage or a crutch to keep you from progressing.

I once met and heard the story of a woman who along with her family had been held hostage for a number of hours. During this time, she was repeatedly molested. When it was over, she moved on with her life. She was often heard to say that those creatures had owned a day of her life. She was not going to let them own the rest of her life. Is this what you have been doing, allowing one incident to own the rest of your life?

While there are times that a little anger can be good, making it a way of life is never good for anyone involved. Take courage and work at identifying the source of it. Please.

For many, fear has managed to creep into their lives in insidious ways. Most of us have been taught to fear from early childhood on. There is the fear of what will happen if we break the rules. That can be a good fear, but there are others that cripple you way down deep. You saw or experienced something that stayed with you and keeps you from growing.

When I was six, my family and I were down at the local swimming hole having a picnic. My older brother went in for a swim. Something went wrong, and he experienced a severe cramp. Suddenly, he was drowning. I remember my father leaping in and dragging him to safety. My mother's reaction to everything left me with a fear of swimming. I would go in the water only so deep. Wading or splashing in the shallow end was enough for me. Of course, I married a man who is an excellent swimmer.

In my late thirties, I decided to face this fear, and enrolled in swimming lessons for adults. While I am not a fantastic swimmer, I know that I have enough skill to conquer that fear and start enjoying myself on outings to the local pool or beach.

What fears are limiting you? Did you have an accident that left you afraid to drive after dark or in certain weather? Did you try something once, when you really were not properly prepared, and not like it or worse yet failed? Were you injured or laughed at?

The point is that now you let that niggling fear take control and direct your life. It may not have anything to do with what really happened in the past. It is there and you let it limit you. Remove any of your fear with faith. Learn to stop being pushed around and controlled by the fears in your mind. Instead, allow yourself to be led by the dreams in your heart. Learn to soar.

Other people watch you and how you handle things—your children and family or friends and coworkers. Whether you want to be or not, you are an example to them. Are you showing them your testimony of faith, or your testimony of fear? Which are you allowing to direct your life? What are you allowing to rub off and affect their lives? What are you speaking so loudly to your children and others through your actions that they may not hear what you are saying verbally? The old line of "Do as I say, not as I do" does not really work.

Along with loving yourself, and consequently others, learning to truly forgive is crucial. At one time or another each of us seeks forgiveness from loved ones, a boss, or from the Lord. It may be for something big or something rather small, but we need to feel forgiven for it before we can allow ourselves to progress.

How often have you denied this same forgiveness to others? Have you ever found yourself saying that you can never forgive so and so for what they did to you or someone you care about? Maybe you withheld forgiveness because you feel that they failed you or embarrassed you deeply. They did not live up to your standards.

Have you ever taken a walk in the woods or high grass and come out with stickers or tiny burrs sticking to your socks or clothing? As you go on, more and more may attach themselves to you until they become a real hindrance to continuing your walk in comfort. You must stop and remove them to progress forward.

When you harbor resentments, old hurts, and misunderstandings, they attach themselves to your spirit. Just like the burrs, they can slow or stop your progression. They may seem insignificant at first but if you do not work to remove or shake some of them off from time to time, they will build up to the point of hurting you. You and your spirit wind up chained to what you do not forgive. You become a prisoner to it. Is it hurting whoever it is aimed at, or is it trapping you? Is that what you want? To truly forgive others is to open the cages of their folly and set yourself free.

I have a very dear friend who was terribly wronged by someone else. Instead of forgiving, the wrong was stuffed down inside. Her soul is still hurting from the wrong. She has allowed it to control part of her life. Instead of going to some activities that she once enjoyed, she now avoids them, so as not to be in close proximity to that person. That person is still going and enjoying themselves. Now, I totally understand my friend's pain. I have felt something similar in my past, as many of you may have. My friend is allowing what happened to limit her activities. In a sense she is the one trapped by what happened, not the wrongdoer. Many people are not being allowed to benefit from my friend's loving and caring ways.

Who are you to deny someone the very thing that you desire most? Just as you wish to be truly loved, you first must love yourself and then others. When you desire to be forgiven, you must first learn to forgive yourself and then forgive others. This is one time when you must put yourself first. If you do not love and forgive yourself, you and your spirit do not have much to give.

Just as loving others must begin with loving yourself first, forgiving others must first begin with completely forgiving yourself. You are not perfect yet. Each of us was sent here to learn perfection. It will not come to us in this life. You may see glimpses of it from time to time to give you hope for what is to come. But it is a lesson we were sent here to work on and progress toward.

You will stumble and fall along the way. That is okay as long as you keep getting back up and moving forward. To stumble and fall does not make you a failure. It is only when you do not get back up that it becomes the problem. As long as you recognize what is blocking your way and what is damaging your soul, you will be able to take steps to remove the blockages and help your soul to heal.

There is much talk about creating peace, wanting world peace, or just longing for peace. One song talks about letting there be peace on earth and letting it begin with me. There is a lot of truth to that. It is a simple fact that as long as you have hatred in your heart, you will never have peace for yourself or anyone else.

Look around you and see how hatred is being stoked and fed to cause unrest, division, and even war. Hatred breeds discord and division between people. Hatred keeps us from learning about others and their cultures. It makes us suspicious and untrusting. It breeds contempt and allows the murdering of others, many of whom are innocent. Hatred controls so much of the world. Do you want it to control your life?

When I was growing up, I was blessed with wise parents. They tried to teach me by example as well as words, to look at another's heart instead of their skin or how they spoke. My father was someone who was welcomed by just about everyone he met. This is something I work to live by and hope that I taught my children. It is what the scriptures teach us. We are all brothers and sisters in the Lord. Some just do not know it yet, and others try to reject it. It is easier to show love and smile than it is to return the distrust and hatred with the same.

"Our paths are all different,
but we walk them together."
Sister Alburto

Part III

Chapter XIV

Defining Yourself

HOW DO YOU DEFINE YOURSELF? Is it by your achievements or by your mistakes? Did you do something that you think you are forever remembered for or defined by? It may have been something like being the kid in the game who got the ball and then scored the winning point. It was just for the opposing side. Maybe you were carrying a tray of coffee to the meeting and tripped causing the coffee to fly all over your boss.

In the scriptures there are examples of people who were caught in a moment of wrongdoing, like the woman caught in adultery. Even though Christ forgave her, she will always be defined by that one act. It does not matter what she may have done with the rest of her life, and it may have been exemplary, she is still defined by that one moment.

Many of us live our lives that way. We define ourselves by some things that we may have done long ago. We obsess about them, replaying them time and again in our minds. We hang on to them and refuse to let go. Why?

There are a lot of different reasons we keep obsessing and beating ourselves up for our mistakes and wrongdoings. Some of them are that we are just hard wired to obsess about them in attempts to either accept the situation that has caused us such pain and trauma or fix it in some way. This negative thinking is a survival tactic. Subconsciously we may think that we can fix ourselves to avoid repeating the problem in the future.

Have you ever had that feeling of wanting to just disappear or shrivel up to nothingness? You would do anything to forget what happened. Why would you ever want to remember such a time? This is exactly what God wants you to do, though. By remembering your mistakes and becoming aware of your weaknesses, you can choose to learn to rely on God for help to avoid future pitfalls. This is where it can become tricky. The adversary likes to use this time to trick you back into obsessing and trapping you into losing your ability to problem solve and forgive yourself. He would have you obsess about your mistakes forever. Jesus Christ wants you to use them to improve the nature of your soul and become more like Him.

So how do you learn to let go? Be willing to take whatever steps are necessary to humble yourself before the Lord and lay your mistakes there. The next step is one that is often overlooked. You are to move forward in faith. You need to leave the past in the past and trust in the Lord that all is made right with Him.

Boyd K. Packer once said, "Purge and cleanse and soothe your soul and your heart and your mind and that of others. A cloud will then be lifted, a beam cast from your eye. There will come that peace which passeth all understanding."

When you come to the Lord with a humble attitude and ask with a sincere desire that the will of the Lord be done. you may rest assured that is now and always the best way.

Remember that Jesus Christ does not define you by who you are or what you may have done, but by what you can ultimately achieve with His guidance and help.

When repentance was mentioned earlier, it did not mean to just say you are sorry and then continue on your way. Sincere repentance requires change on your part—change about how you think about some things, and how you behave. You may have to change how you view some things and how you let them affect you.

What you have always done or how you have viewed things has brought you to this point. That is what has weakened and drained your soul and your body. Try looking at it this way. Learning a new way, new mental and spiritual skills, can give you a different perspective on the world around you. Life can become a grand adventure. I love adventures. How about you?

Which are you: a pessimist or an optimist? Do you know the difference? Winston Churchill once said, "A Pessimist sees the difficulty in every opportunity. An Optimist sees the opportunity in every difficulty." What do you do?

You are probably familiar with the childhood characters from Winnie the Pooh. There is poor old Eeyore, who sees all the reasons not to do something. All the "what ifs." A lot of the time he is so busy doing that, that he does not see all the love and beauty around him. Fortunately, he has friends who care and work to include him.

Then you have Tigger. Tigger is so full of energy and happiness, that he just bounds all over the place. He puts a smile on everyone's face. Granted, he does not always think things through, but he enjoys the adventure.

These are two extreme opposites, but you get the picture. Eeyore is depressed and worried all the time. He does not exhibit any faith in anything or anyone around him. It hurts him and hampers his enjoyment and growth. He fails to recognize any opportunity in his difficulty.

Tigger seems to see opportunity all around him and overlooks any difficulty. All he seems to see is the beauty life has to offer. Lots of times he winds up in trouble that his friends must guide him out of. Do you know any people who seem to fit into either of these categories?

As you go through life, it is alright to recognize the possible difficulties and pitfalls that are there. That is just good sense. It is when you allow them to bring a screeching halt to your growth and healing that they become a real problem.

You may be asking how to go about finding a middle ground between these two extremes. What are you supposed to do to let go of the fears of the future, and yet not go off on a wild tangent that gets you into some type of difficulty? The answer may seem rather simplistic, but it does work. Pray about everything and worry about nothing. You are not in this alone. Prayer will give you comfort and sometimes direction. Scriptures will give you guidance.

It does not matter how you were raised. Whether church was an integral part of your upbringing or not. Maybe you grew up in a "send the children to church, instead of taking them to church" home. Perhaps you were dragged to church every Sunday, whether you felt like going or not. Maybe church and God were not even part of your life. However you were raised is not the question now. You are beginning to build a new you. When a person starts to build anything, it is important to set a firm foundation. This platform keeps the structure from collapsing when life gets rough. One of the most important parts of your new foundation is making God a cornerstone. He helps us build a firm foundation.

Some of you may protest and say that you have done just fine without bringing God into it. Have you? What were you searching for when you started this book? What has been lacking all those years? How has life shaken and taken its toll on you and your spirit? Now is the time to try something different, so that you may heal and find your purpose in this life.

How do you go about finding God and inviting Him into your life? One small step at a time. How do you know that He will welcome you? Open your heart, and you will feel a warmth, or a comfort that has been missing for a very long time. If you do not really try, you will never know.

Read and study the scriptures themselves. Do not read what someone else has had to say about them and God. Find out for yourself. Read them and then pray to know if they are true. Build that foundation of faith deep in your heart so that you will have the strength and power to endure when life comes around to knock you down.

Here I am recommending that you start praying, without giving you a real understanding as to what real prayer is.

Prayer is a sincere communication between you and the Lord. Notice, I said communication. That means that it goes both ways. Just as you hope that He listens and hears your prayers, you must open yourself to listening for the answers.

History shows that before the first generation of man had passed away, men were calling upon the name of the Lord, sometimes with sacrifices and sometimes without. The ancient patriarchs constantly prayed. It has never been put forth as a duty, but it has been constantly used down through the ages.

There have been and still are those who pray from the rooftops or loudly in public or in the streets. Some may open an eye to see who is witnessing their piety. In my humble opinion, that is not real prayer.

It is when you become aware and learn the true relationship you have with God (namely that God is your father and you are his beloved child) that prayer can become natural and instinctive. It is only when you forget this that difficulties can arise with your prayers.

During this sincere communication between you and the Lord, your will and His are brought into correspondence with each other. It is not meant to try to change God's will, but to draw closer to Him and learn His will.

There are so many blessings that are waiting for you. Imagine if you will, of walking through heaven with a guide. You are shown one fantastic thing after another. Some individuals seem to be so blessed and others are not. This makes you wonder some. Your guide, sensing your thoughts, takes you to an immense warehouse. Inside are shelves upon shelves of packages stacked as high as you can see. You look in wonder upon them and ask what they are. The guide smiles rather sadly and explains that each package is a blessing that our Heavenly Father has for each of us. The only thing that keeps us from receiving them is that we have not asked to secure these blessings for ourselves and others.

All blessings require some work on your part. Prayer and belief are forms of this work and leads to the highest of blessings.

Many prayers may go unanswered. To receive these blessings and to get answers, all prayers must be offered in the name of Jesus Christ. When you do not pray in His Holy Name, you are not aligning yourself with His mind or will.

You can choose to pray in solitude, away from any distractions. Sometimes you may pray with a loved one, standing or kneeling together. You may be asked to give a prayer aloud or to pray over a gathering. There are many scenarios. The most important thing is to learn to pray in the name of Jesus Christ and to listen for the answers you seek.

These answers can come from unexpected places and at different times. They may come from something someone says or does. They may come in a piece of scripture you read or in a hymn or other pieces of music you hear. Learn to look for them. Sometimes they come as a subtle prompting or a prodding to do something.

This is an example from my own life. Once, we had moved to a place where the range was in bad need of being replaced. There had been a fire in the oven and half the burners did not work. I turned the problem over to the Lord in prayer. Several months later I was exploring a neighboring small town with my children. As I was pulling out of a parking lot, I felt the prompting to pull into the small lot across the street and go into a little appliance store that was there. When I entered the store a kind gentleman asked if he could assist me. I told him that I was looking for a drop-in electric range. He led me over to one that people had decided they did not want after having ordered it. It was marked down to the price I had decided we could spend. It was the right size to fit where the old one was. Everything fit into the parameters that I had to work within. A true answer to a prayer. I just had to heed the promptings.

When used right, prayer is an unbelievably valuable gift. Our spirits are not only healed but nurtured by the eternal truths we find when we turn to our Heavenly Father.

The idea of a Heavenly Father who loves and cares for you may be difficult for some to imagine. In many homes the father figure is not there for one reason or another. The parents may have split up. The father may be away for employment or he just might be totally disconnected from his family. Your feelings may be that if your earthly father does not care about you, how can you even imagine that a heavenly one is even there much less caring about you. You do not really have a good point of reference. This is going to require a total change of your thinking to come to accept that Heavenly Father loving and caring about you is very real.

When you open your heart and mind to the truth, you will find an acceptance that will comfort and guide you to more truths. To learn truth, is to find God. You see, Heavenly Father is the father of our souls. The soul is nourished and nurtured by the eternal truths. Prayer cleanses the soul and strengthens it. Isn't that one of the things you have been seeking?

God, our Heavenly Father, has always been there. He is the same yesterday, today and tomorrow. You are the one who isn't. Day-to-day happenings can distance us from God. That is the reason why you must seek Him each day and strive to grow more like Him. Treasure the time you spend seeking Him. It is said that where your treasure is, so is your heart.

Your journey on this earth is so much more than getting to your destination. It is the journey itself. Once upon a time, long before your memories begin, you agreed to come on this journey. You left the comfort of heaven and came here to embark on this great adventure. Now all adventures run into peril, some more than others. You look around and hope to find a way out. You may feel alone and helpless. God has not left you to fight on your own. He is there for every step you take. His presence is in every breath and every action you take. He is there to sustain you on your journey, no matter how perilous it may seem. You do not have to hope that He is there. All you have to do is open your heart and your eyes to see His abundance and love. The Lord is with you and all around you now. Not sometime in the future, but in the miracle of now. Remember the warehouse? All you have to do is ask in the name of Jesus Christ for those gifts to be given to you.

Faith grows within you a little day by day as you seek out your Heavenly Father. You are discovering a way to heal and grow upon. When this plan becomes embedded in your heart, you will have the power to endure all things without crumbling. You will have the power to walk through the storms of life with your head up and your heart strong. An old song talks about climbing every mountain. Life is filled with so many mountains in different shapes and heights. Through faith you will be able to surmount each one.

As your spirit grows stronger and you feel the healing, there is more that you can do to show your gratitude than just keep a journal. Look around and see where you may help someone else who is lost. This is called service.

I once heard service described as the rent we pay for being here on earth. I prefer to think of it more as helping others who are lost and hurting, just as someone reached out and helped you.

When you find something that brings you joy, happiness, and peace, don't you want to share it with others? Joy and happiness seem to increase when shared. It is like the smile that makes another smile. Or the laugh that draws others to laugh as well, even when they have no idea what is so funny. I promise that you will only grow stronger as you share with others.

You may feel that your schedule is already full. Where will you find time to share and help others? You are not expected to quit work and go live in the slums somewhere ministering to the poor. It is more like having your light shine so bright that others will want what you have. When they ask you about it, listen to them and then tell them.

Where are you supposed to find places to serve? Look around. Offer forgiveness when someone misses the mark. Thank someone for just being there. Does someone live near you who is alone? Reach out to them. Your overtures may not be welcomed at first, but you are never wrong when you are doing what is right.

Keep in mind that it is important to make sure that your daily activities allow time for communication with the Lord. This will strengthen you and your soul. It puts the entire day into perspective. It helps you to find and recognize your purpose. As you learn to love God with all your heart, you will find that He turns your heart toward the well-being of others in a very beautiful and virtuous way.

One of my favorite parts in the New Testament is found in Matthew 25:35 - 40. "For I was hungered, and you gave me meat: I was thirsty, and you gave me drink: I was a stranger, and you took me in: Naked, and you clothed me: I was sick, and ye visited me…Then shall the righteous answer him, saying, 'Lord, when saw we thee and hungered, and fed thee? Or thirsty, and gave thee drink? When saw we thee a stranger, and took thee in? Or naked, and clothed thee? And when saw we thee sick, or in prison, and came unto thee?'

And the King shall answer and say unto them, 'Verily I say unto you, inasmuch as ye have done it unto the least of these my brethren, ye have done it unto me.'"

This does not mean that you should go around beating your chest and showing how good you are to be helping others. Do it quietly, sometimes in secret. A line from a favorite hymn, "Love One Another," states "try to show kindness in all that you do." Simple directions to follow. Quiet acts of service may not get you much recognition, but they will give you much satisfaction and spread joy and comfort to others. Your actions are what people see and relate to. Sincerely listen to others and talk to them, not at them. Your actions are what will help other souls to find strength and healing.

Back in the 1980s there seemed to be a type of revival where many people were "born again" Christians. They were very proud of it and proclaimed it to all who would listen. I heard one person point out that these people were so busy being "born again" that they never got out of the delivery room and got down to the day to day living as a child of the Lord. I understand their excitement of having found and accepted the Lord into their hearts. That is one of the most wonderful things that can happen, but unless they start to back it up with study and prayer their newfound joy will fade. Just like a baby, it needs to be fed and nurtured. Scripture study, prayer, and service feeds and nourishes that joy and discovery.

Have you ever noticed that every time you get something in life, that 'something' requires care and some of your time? You have received an incredibly special gift from your Heavenly Father. Your soul is healed and filled with more happiness than it knows what to do with. Now, you must take the steps necessary to keep it strong and well. In the scriptures, several times there is the statement of "It is well with my soul." Not well with my body. Not well with my mind. But "well with my soul." Your soul is no longer on life support!

Do not get disappointed when you look in the mirror and outwardly you may still look the same. You may still be heavier than you would like to be, or still need glasses, or whatever. Now look closer and see the lightness that comes from within. The peace that seems to surround you. That is what healing the soul does to a person.

Now that you have found how to heal your soul and allowed it to become well and strong, I must tell you that the battle is not over. Learning to protect and continue to nourish the soul is an ongoing task.

Our souls are older than our bodies. You were a spirit child in heaven before you agreed to come down to earth. You listened and learned about the wonderful plan that Heavenly Father has for each of us. It was exciting and good, so you chose to accept an earthly body and come down here to earth.

When you accepted this challenge, you also entered into a struggle or battle for your soul. You have since found that the great adversary, Satan, is the enemy of your spirit. Make no mistake, he wants you to fail. He attacks you through the desires and appetites of your body.

The followers in some cults, through the ages, have gone without food and flogged themselves to try to overcome those desires and appetites. They have closed themselves off from society and hidden from the world. This is not what Christ would have you do.

You are to be in this world, not of it. That means that you are to be out here with the rest of us, living and sharing and striving to do and be good. You may stumble like the rest of us. Get up, take a breath and go on. Never give up.

"Be not thou therefore ashamed of
the testimony of Our Lord..."

2 Timothy 1:8

Chapter XV

Staying Strong

MAKE NO MISTAKE, SATAN IS still out there. He is still hoping that you fail. To do that, he is using all he has to make that happen. The most effective tool that he uses is fear. It is all around you and is not new. When Jesus' disciples were out on the Sea of Galilee and a storm came up, they feared the wind and the waves and the dark of night.

Things have not changed much today. As you have been healing and growing, you may have encountered times when your newfound peace and faith have been questioned or challenged. This is not new and is not happening to just you. In 2 Timothy 1:8 we are instructed "Be not thou therefore ashamed of the testimony of our Lord…" I like to put in the word fear for ashamed, but it is clear that you are to let your light shine forth and not hide it because of fear.

Even with this newfound strength of spirit, you will be beset with different fears. It is just how Satan works. If you are single, he will beset you with fears of commitment and marriage. Or the opposite of not being chosen and being single all your life.

Once you are married, there is the fear of bringing children into this hard and wicked world. Should you have them? Will they be healthy and okay? Will you be a good parent?

When you are sharing and ministering, you may face the fear of approaching strangers or having your efforts rejected. Remember that being rejected has nothing to do with your value, but more to do with where the other person is on their journey. Sometimes they just are not in a position to recognize or accept what is offered with love.

If you are widowed or divorced, you may feel the fear of having to go forward alone. Be assured that the Lord is with you every step of the way and will lead and protect you. He will give you comfort.

You may look back on when you were a child and how you feared the first day of school. As you got older, you may have feared getting back your test results. When you left home for the first time, there were a number of fears assaulting you.

Each of us faces different fears. Fear of rejection, failure, and disappointment. Are we good enough, smart enough, strong enough? Then there is the fear of the great unknown.

Listening to the news can bring fear of the storms, tornados, hurricanes, earthquakes. and fires that you have no power over. You know how they can ravage your life or the lives of your loved ones.

What if you do not get chosen, but on the other hand what if you are chosen.

You may fear that the Lord has no blessings left for you.

The changes that are happening around and to you can make you uncomfortable and fearful. Please do not let those fears escalate into anxiety or terror. The Lord is always with you, no matter what.

Do you realize how much fear limits and colors your perspective? In 2 Kings you will find the story of the prophet Elisha. The Syrian king had sent a legion of soldiers to surround the city by night so they could capture and kill Elisha.

When Elisha's servant went out in the morning, he saw the soldiers surrounding the city and went back to Elisha with much fear. He asked what they were to do. He was letting the fear speak.

Elisha answered him "Fear not: for they that be with us are more than they that be with them." Then he prayed that the Lord would open the eyes of his servant.

When the servant opened his eyes, he saw a mountain of horses and chariots of fire round about Elisha.

While you probably do not have those chariots of fire to dispel your fears, the lesson is clear. The Lord is with you, and mindful of you. He is blessing you in ways that only He can. When you pray, you are calling down the strength and revelation that you need. It helps you to center your thoughts on Jesus Christ and His atoning sacrifice. He knows that you will have fears to face. Because of His great sacrifice for each of us, he has faced every fear that you have or can have. He counsels us to "Be of good cheer; it is I; be not afraid." Matthew 14:27 "O thou of little faith, therefore didst thou doubt?" Matthew 14:31.

Deuteronomy 31:8 assures you "And the Lord, he it is that doth go before thee, he will be with thee, he will not fail thee; neither forsake thee: fear not, neither be dismayed."

One of my personal favorites is "The Lord is my rock, and my fortress, and my deliverer." 2 Samuel 22:10. I testify that Christ lives. Your love for Him and His gospel will dispel each of your fears.

Each day strive to grow closer to the Lord. It is about learning to live a "guided" life. A few years ago, there was a good fad. People, young people in particular, were wearing WWJD bracelets. They were meant to remind each of them of "What Would Jesus Do" when they were confronted with what life throws at them. This is sound advice. There really is no right way to do what you know is wrong. Conversely, there is no wrong way to do what you know to be right. Strive to keep that in mind when you are faced with different trials.

In this world you have to be constantly vigilant for the hidden attacks that will distract you. At first, they may appear to be genuinely nice, desirable, pleasant, and attractive. You need to become aware of the beguiling bad that appears to be good. In Isaiah we are warned "Woe unto them that call evil good, and good evil; that put darkness for light, and light for darkness; that put bitter for sweet, and sweet for bitter." Even though that verse was written thousands of years ago, its message seems to fit our current world. How wonderful it is that we have scriptures to guide us and help us recognize the adversary's dark attractions, distractions, and deceptions.

In these modern times it is easy to be distracted by all of the gadgets and electronics. A minute to check your email can turn into an hour before you realize it. Your time gets eaten up and there is no time left to study scriptures or pray. You tell yourself that you will do it later. Later never comes and you become complacent and casual about your relationship with the Lord. He is still there, but you have moved away and not kept a place for Him in your life. This thoughtlessness can put you in grave danger from the adversary. Your life and your soul are at risk.

Constant vigilance is required to prevent you from falling into complacency and casualness in your relationship with the Lord. You need to learn to be on continual watch for possible dangers and difficulties. This is when it is good to know and understand how to recognize the prompting from the Holy Spirit and signals you may receive that all is not well. This does not mean that you are to go around constantly fearful. Be alert and pray often. I once read this sound advice: "Pray about everything, and fear nothing." This can increase your capacity to look and listen when you might not think you need to.

When you seek to learn and do the will of the Lord, you come to recognize that Satan is the enemy of all righteousness. He is continually working and striving to make you, a child of God, as miserable as he is. He labors to make you confused and unhappy and distant from your Heavenly Father. He will work diligently to attack your faith and your soul. He hates the Lord and the Lord's plans for you. He will do all in his power to draw you away. You and your soul's safety lie in never allowing yourself to be led into that first step away. Keep working at doing what you should do.

The adversary will attack you through your appetites. You will be tempted to drink things you shouldn't and eat things that you should stay away from. You may be tempted to watch, listen to, or read things, that while they are enticing and feel good for the moment, will only lead you away from what is good and right. Understanding the intent of these attacks is vital to being prepared to repel them and be victorious. When you are prepared, you have nothing to fear.

How are you supposed to recognize when the Lord is trying to tell you something? It can be exceedingly difficult sometimes to recognize the difference between your own thoughts and the gentle impressions from the Lord. What are you to do? Scriptures instruct us that if something invites and lures you to do good, it comes from Christ. Think about what you are doing. Does it give you peace? Do you get a good feeling deep inside? You are on the right track. Learn to recognize that feeling and direction.

Make sure that you carve out time each day to study and draw closer to God. It is too easy to be distracted by noises and routines even in your own home. These things can occupy your mind and your heart leaving no room to learn what the gentle prompting from the Lord feels like.

Generally, the Lord will reveal and communicate with you in private. It may be in your room, on a quiet walk, just some place away from all the noises and tumult.

The noise and tumult make it hard to hear the Lord's still, small voice. The adversary knows that and works to keep you away from the quiet places. Choose a time and place and learn to listen for God's voice every day.

When you hear those promptings, act on them right away. Years ago, I received a prompting to call a dear friend back in a state we had moved from. It was at a time when you still had to pay long distance charges, so I was tempted to put it off until the rates dropped. As I stepped away from the phone, it was like a force was standing in front of me blocking my way. Once again, I felt that I needed to call my friend. The feeling was so very strong that I dialed her number. I will never forget what her first words were to me. "I am so glad you called. I was sitting here thinking about killing myself." The promptings you receive may not be so dramatic, but they are just as important and vital for you.

While you are working at keeping your soul strong and well, the adversary is working just as hard to make sure you fail. He has three tools that he likes to use against each of us.

The first is deception. Remember that you are a child of God. The adversary is relentless to make you forget that. He seeks to make you feel less than that. One of his goals is to make you worship him. The scriptures tell you that you were created in God's own image and that He has work for you to do. Satan tries to deceive you into forgetting who you really are. When you recognize your true identity, then you can realize who you can become.

The second tool is distraction. The adversary attempts to distract you away from God and the path you are to follow. His design is to distract you from the spiritual, while the Lord's desire is to enlighten you and engage you in His work.

You have plenty of things from Facebook to Twitter, to virtual games to distract you. Technological advances are amazing, but if you are not careful, they will distract you from finding your divine purpose. When used wisely they can bring forth the powers of heaven and allow you to witness miracles as you seek to find other like-minded souls. Be careful and cautious in your use of technology. Look for ways that it can be used to draw you closer to your Savior. Isaiah 5:20 teaches "Woe unto them that call evil good."

I have saved what I consider the biggest one for last. It is discouragement. Satan loves it when you get discouraged. There are so many ways that he uses to do this.

Do you get discouraged when something does not fit? You look around and compare yourself to others. You are not slim enough, pretty enough. You feel like your home is not nice enough. What are others thinking of you? You are not smart enough or worst of all that you are not worthy of God's love and acceptance. This happens when you compare yourself to others. You feel that you are not living up to expectations including your own.

Stop comparing yourself to some imagined image. Stop trying to live up to unreasonable expectations. Do not let anyone, including yourself, rob you of your peace and happiness. Christ left you with this message. "Peace I leave unto you; not as the world giveth, give I unto you. Let not your heart be troubled, neither let it be afraid." John 14:27.

How are you going to overcome the deception, distraction, and discouragement that the adversary throws at you? There are several steps you can take.

First is to remember the first great commandment that is to love God with your heart, mind, and strength. Let this love for Him and Jesus Christ motivate all that you do. As you do this and keep His commandments you will find that your capacity to love others and yourself increases. As you serve and help family, friends, and neighbors, you will start to see them as the Savior sees them. We are all sons and daughters of our Heavenly Father, your brothers and sisters.

Secondly, pray in the name of Jesus Christ every day. Through prayer, you will begin to feel God's love for you and demonstrate your love for Him. Through prayer, you learn to express gratitude. You can ask for strength and guidance. You learn to submit your will to His will and start to live that guided life.

Thirdly, read and study your scriptures every day. I like to do mine at the beginning of my day. It makes me feel as if I am prepared or armed for what is ahead of me. If you have a question, try to read your scriptures with it in mind. That will help you receive revelation and guidance. Yes, you may receive your own personal revelations.

Remember the sacrifice that Christ made for you in the garden at Gethsemane and his sacrifice on the cross. That was for you. Show your gratitude by keeping the Commandments and always remembering Him. This is how you achieve a peaceful soul and an abundant life. Jesus declared, "I am come that they might have life, and that they might have it more abundantly." John 10:10.

You may ask, how do you achieve this abundant life? The answer is simple, but probably not what you are looking for. The answer to achieving an abundant life is in service to others and becoming a true disciple of Christ. By learning of and following His ways and engaging in His work you will find it. Believe in Christ, love Him as He loved, and follow His prompting. Reach out to others and do not judge them or their circumstances. Share with others the truths that you have found. Spread the Gospel of Christ in all that you do. That does not mean to stand on a box on some street corner shouting scriptures at passersby. It means to let your light shine. Be kind and thoughtful of others. Fill their needs when you can. By doing these things, your own troubles and pains will soften, and your soul will be filled with exceedingly great joy.

This may seem like an oversimplification, but you are basically being asked to believe in God and Jesus Christ. Follow up on this belief by loving others as He loves you. Then do what you are being led to do and serve others. You may feel that all of the ills around you are much too complex to be taken care of by something so simple. Do you remember how to eat an elephant? One bite at a time. By loving and believing, you learn that it is the love of God that does it all. That love rescues, restores, and revives.

God loves you, even when you may think that you are beyond being loveable. He reaches out to you. All you have to do is take His hand and walk with Him.

He will fill the emptiness in you and give you joy and comfort. Those dark clouds over you will part. You will look up and see the brilliant light of His unending glory.

Many go through life thinking that they are too educated, intelligent, or experienced to believe in such nonsense. They do not need to believe in some unseen deity or old foolish traditions. They know too much to believe in a living God, let alone that He loves them. They just can't and won't see it. In some respects, they are not far wrong. The scriptures teach "that without faith, it is impossible to please Him: for he that cometh to God must believe that he is." Hebrews 11:6.

I have been taught that faith is believing in things yet unseen. It is not about discussing and theorizing about one point or another. Believing takes some blood, sweat and tears. By them, the seeds are planted, and the fruit ripens and remains in your heart and soul. As you draw nearer to the Lord, He will draw nearer to you. This is a promise to you when you seek to have faith and believe.

When you love God and His other children deeply and unconditionally, the happier you will become. By love, I do not mean the convenient spoken and then forgotten words. It is the kind that enters your heart the moment you wake up and stays with you all day. It swells your heart and warms you as you prayerfully give gratitude at your days end. This gives you an idea of how your Heavenly Father loves you.

When you are filled with this love and compassion, you begin to truly see others. You recognize them as beings of infinite potential and worth. You see that they are also beloved daughters and sons of Heavenly Father. Once the lens of your vision is cleared, it becomes hard to discriminate against or disregard anyone again.

You reach out in love to others because it is what the Savior wants you to do. Your seemingly small efforts will have eternal consequences. Many times, the simple things that you do, your daily efforts, will be taken and used for something miraculous. It can be wonderful when you find yourself being used in this way. In a sense you become a ministering angel to someone in need. Do not be surprised. Angels can come in all shapes, sizes, and forms.

Reaching out to others is more than just being nice to them. Being nice is a good start. When you listen to the promptings from above and prayerfully seek to serve, you will be led in the ways that comfort, teach and lead. It is much like becoming a shepherd.

A shepherd watches over his flock and knows each sheep. Depending on the size of his flock, he may have others who assist him. Some of them are experienced old-timers and others may be learning the ins and outs of shepherding. When the flock is counted, there may be losses. It is usually some of the young lambs that have wandered away from the safety of the flock. They can become victims of the ever-present predators in wait. Are you able to see the similarities with our human lives?

Jesus often referred to himself as the good shepherd. He said that He knows each of His flock by name and will lay down His life for them. Before His arrest and crucifixion, Jesus told Peter to feed his sheep three times. It was that important. You may have been taught to pray that the Lord is your shepherd. What do you think was meant by that?

When the storms of life come with the winds, rain or snowstorms that rage around you and the illnesses, injuries and other trials, the Lord, your Shepherd, will bring you through. He will minister to you and heal your soul. Sometimes you are called upon to assist in tending the flock. You have a responsibility to reach out and serve others as you have been served. You reach out in love to others because it is what the Savior has commanded you to do.

When you see your neighbor in distress in one way or another, you go to their aid. You offer comfort and assistance. You mourn with them and sometimes laugh with them, helping to lighten their load where you can.

You may not know this, but sheep are far from being the smartest of animals.

If one goes out in a storm, the others will try to follow. They will shy and bolt or run off at a sudden noise. Herding and protecting them takes constant vigilance. One of the duties of the shepherd is to find the ones who have strayed before they have gone too far and become prey.

Many times, someone who is newly found and healed will start to feel lonesome and maybe start to feel as if they do not belong. This is when, just like a sheep, they will go out in the storm or turn away. They will seek out old ways that led them to be in need of help in the first place. You are instructed from on high to search for and reach out to them. Bring them back to the fold and surround them with friends. Show them how much they are needed. Learn to be flexible in your ways. What works for one, may not work the same way for another.

Just as I hope you have learned that you are very loved and precious to your Heavenly Father, so are others. He loves each of us with a love that is so big, you cannot even begin to fathom. He sees immeasurable potential in each of His children. It is like when you look at your child and see all the good that you wish for them. Just as you will stand by them through all the good and the bad, He is there to protect and lead each of us through the storms. Sometimes, you will be one of His aids to find and minister to the ones who have strayed and are in need of being loved back in.

You may have never thought of yourself as being an angel or a shepherd to someone else, but often the Lord will use you in just that way.

"You hold in your hands the happiness
of more people than you can imagine"
Henry B. Eyring

Chapter XVI

Maintenance

WHEN YOU HAVE A CAR, you know that every few months it needs to go for a checkup and an assessment of how it is running. What needs changed or replaced and what just needs a little fine tuning? While this can be an inconvenience, it is better than being broken down on the side of the road. It is the same way with your life.

Periodically, you need to step back and assess how you are doing. It is easy to get so caught up in all the distractions and information overloads that you forget to tune in to how you are doing. Unless you take the time to step back and do a maintenance check, you may not realize how much impact the fast-paced environment is having on your life and your decisions. All of the information coming at you in the forms of glaring headlines, entertaining videos and other memes may be interesting and informative, but are most of them helping you on your walk with the Lord? They may be slyly eating away at your day leaving no time for you to nurture your soul. How much do you let them shape your judgements and the way you experience life? In Luke 21:34 we are cautioned to "take heed...lest at any time your hearts be overcharged with...cares of life."

I have always wondered about the phrase that "many will be called but few are chosen." It means that the ones who are not chosen have their hearts set upon the things of the world. They aspire to all the honors of men.

When you step back from the world and assess where you are in your walk with the Lord, it gives you an opportunity to replace or correct some things that may be leading you astray. It is a time to reflect and fine tune where you are on your path—to get a clearer image of where you are headed and a forward perspective on it. While doing this assessment you may ask yourself about how you can rise above the distractions of this world and keep nourishing and protecting your soul.

One way is to learn to prioritize the choices you make. What choices are good for you? What choices are better for you? Which is the best one for you? The first two tiers are the ones that help you develop faith in the Lord and strengthen your spirit. The absolute best choices, however, are centered on Jesus Christ and learning the truths of who He is and who you are in your relationship with Him. Some may find this to be rather restricting, but John 8:31-32 teaches "If ye continue in my word, then ye are my disciples indeed: And ye shall know the truth, and the truth shall make you free."

I once heard a Christian comic talk about how some of his acquaintances complained about all the "thou shalt nots" in the Bible. I agree there are a lot of them. The comic went on to point out that there are really more directions on what you should be doing. As he then stated, "If you get busy doing all the do's, you don't have time for the don't."

As you step back into this swiftly moving world that seems to be moving to alternative realities, please remember that the spirit speaks only truth. It does not lie. Your spirit will recognize how things really are. Listen to it. Decide what changes you need to make.

It is good that your soul is healing and growing stronger all the time and that you have a growing faith in the Lord. You read about receiving spiritual gifts and all the wonderful things that are out there. These are all good things, but faith takes action to continue to grow.

Let's look at it this way. You can read about all the muscles in your body, learning about them and all the things they are designed to do. It is truly fascinating, but just reading about them is not going to make your muscles stronger or give them definition.

The amazing gift of faith is so much more than an idea or a mood. It is more than a feeling. I have often heard or read that faith without action does very little. When you live your faith and follow the promptings, you may be surprised by the results.

Other people watch you, especially when you have shared that you are a Christian. They are not necessarily waiting for you to mess up, but they are learning from your example. Through your actions, some of them may receive the precious gift of hope. In serving others, you will often forget about yourself and your own problems. When you return to those problems, they will seem small compared to what you have witnessed, or they have gone away.

Do you know about the unassuming little mustard seed? It is a relatively small seed. When planted in fertile ground, it will grow quickly, and grow and grow until it is a large enough plant that birds build their nests in it. I think that this is why your faith is often compared to a mustard seed. It will start out small, but with care and feeding it will grow. The winds that buffet it and the storms that rage around it are exercises to make it stronger. Your faith can grow like that mustard seed.

Have you noticed that when a person is given something without doing anything to earn it, that the gift is not always fully appreciated? It is that way with spiritual gifts. Heavenly Father knows that you treasure things that you have to earn. He will give you opportunities to develop those gifts. When you are in tune, and act upon these opportunities, the gifts grow stronger. They may be things that you never realized were there.

I have learned over the years to be careful what I ask for in the way of gifts. Patience has always been a problem for me. When I asked for patience, I learned about having to wait for some things and putting the needs of others in front of my own. I learned to accept that the Lord's timing is perfect. To have more love in my life, I had to offer more to others, in both my family and sometimes to people I did not know well. Have I learned or received patience? Most of the time, I can answer "yes" to that question. Sometimes my soul may be feeling overburdened, and I need to learn from another's patience.

Exercising faith can be very similar. When doubts start coming to mind, and they will, you will find yourself having to trust in the Lord's promises so that you may continue moving forward. This is one more way to exercise those spiritual muscles and develop them into sources of strength in your life.

You may have already found that it is not the easiest in the beginning. It may even be a challenge for you. It is just like exercising the body. At first, the body is not very strong, and it may ache and complain. You keep at it and find that your body has grown stronger over time. It is this way with your faith. Some scriptures tell you that when you come to the Lord, He will first show you your weaknesses. They have been given to you so that you may become humble. Humble is another word for teachable. God's grace is sufficient for all who become humble before the Lord. When you become teachable and have faith in the Lord, you will be made strong.

Please identify those spiritual muscles that need a bit more exercise than others and work on them with more spiritual activity. Life is more of a marathon than a sprint. This is why it is important to engage in spiritual activities that will keep you strong. If you want to increase your faith and strengthen it, do things that require faith. Sometimes that may mean stepping into the darkness and taking the light of your faith with you. Just stay connected to your light source, Jesus Christ.

Earlier, we talked about that great warehouse filled with blessings that people never ask for. There is a little more to it than that. Imagine a very large wood pile with nice small pieces of kindling piled in the middle. Just so you know, kindling are small pieces that are dry and will easily catch fire. These may be topped with larger wood chips and then small branches and larger logs. On top are huge logs that are capable of burning for days and producing heat and light. Next to this enormous pile is a single small match. For all the energy in the pile of wood to be released, that match needs to be struck and put into the kindling. This is a small action that will release the energy in that pile of wood.

There are several variables that can affect this. The match might not light. If it does light, it might not be applied to the kindling. If oxygen is not there in the form of a slight breeze or you blowing on it, the kindling might not catch.

This is how it is when the Lord desires to give you blessings. It requires action on your part based on your faith in the Lord. This is the first action that is required. Faith in Jesus Christ is a principle of action and power. When you act in faith, the power comes according to the Lord's timing and will. Your faith may be tiny like that little match but when used the blessings you receive will be great.

Are you familiar with the story of fiery serpents attacking the Israelites on their march to the promised land? The bite of these serpents was deadly. Moses was instructed to form a brass serpent and place it on a staff so that it could be seen by all. People were told to look upon this brass serpent and be healed. How hard was that?

Those who followed the instructions were given access to the healing powers of heaven and were instantly healed. Others would not look and died. Maybe they lacked the faith to look. Perhaps they were like many who can't understand how doing something so simple could possibly work, or their hearts were too hardened and their souls too weak to even listen to a prophet's voice.

Like the ancient Israelites, you must act on your faith to be blessed. This is a heavenly law decreed from the very beginning of this world, that when you receive any blessings from the Lord, it is by obedience to having faith in Him. You do not earn blessings, but you do have to qualify for them. Your faith is like that tiny match that lit a fire that could be seen for miles. Even heaven sees it, because of those little acts of faith that were required to light the Lord's promises.

To receive a blessing act with faith. That starts with prayer. Did you realize that one of the objects of prayer is to ask for what blessings the Lord is ready to grant to you? Praying is an act of faith. The activation of energy, or lighting the wood pile, is needed from you to have enough faith in Jesus Christ to sincerely ask the Lord in prayer and then accept His will and timing. Sometimes your ongoing faith filled actions are required as well. Sometimes you need to continue in actions and prayer before the blessings come.

Heavenly Father is aware of you and your needs. Probably more than you are. He will send perfect help. Sometimes it comes right away as soon as you ask, almost. Sometimes your most earnest and worthy desires are not answered in the time and way that you had hoped. If you are patient, you may find that Heavenly Father has something even greater in store for you. Sometimes you may have to wait until the next life.

The following are several ways in which your prayers may be answered. You have saved and budgeted to purchase a new outfit that you found online. It looked so pretty in the picture. You prayed about a new look that would help you get that promotion you want and feel you have earned. When it finally arrives, the outfit is not right for you. The way it fits is not as flattering as you thought it would be. It just does not feel comfortable. You set the outfit aside with the intent of returning it as soon as you get around to it. A week or so later a friend calls you, almost in tears. You are aware that she had lost her job several months before and has been struggling. You invite her to come over for a nice talk. When she arrives, you learn that she has a good job interview lined up for the next day, but literally has nothing to wear to it. Her one good interview suit caught in a door and now has a big tear in a very obvious place. It is then that you remember that outfit you had ordered and offer it to her. She tries it on, and It fits her well and will be perfect for the interview. She promises to pay you for it after she lands the job. It does not matter; her prayer was answered. The next week, a birthday present arrives from your mother. It is a new outfit that is exactly right for you. Your prayer was answered.

Heavenly Father knew that your friend was going to need something to wear for that interview, but that she had no means to go out and buy something. He also knew that your new outfit was not right for you, but that it would be an answer to your friend's urgent prayer and immediate need.

There may be situations where your very worthy desires are not granted to you, or at least not in the way you had hoped. Take heart. It is for your ultimate good. You have met someone special. They appear to be everything you have been hoping and praying for. Oh, how you want this to last and grow into something wonderful, but it doesn't. You are heartbroken but pick yourself up and keep going. Much later, you find out from a mutual friend that your special person has been arrested on some terrible felony charge. Your prayer not being answered the way you hoped was really a blessing to you. You were kept from a great danger.

You have worked hard, studied harder, and prepared for a position with a well-respected company. You have prayed and are feeling confident that you will be hired. The interview goes well, and you are called back for a second one. This is really looking good for you, but the position goes to someone else. You wonder "why." Several days later your current boss offers you a new position with more pay and responsibility, and you accept. It was not what you had prayed for, but it is good. Months later, you read the headline that the CEO of the company you had interviewed with has been arrested for embezzling funds from his company. Once again, your prayers were answered to your best benefit. God knows the end from the beginning, and in situations like I just described, the answer to your righteous prayers was no, in favor of something far more superior for you.

Have you ever known someone with a physical affliction, like deafness or being wheelchair bound? You may have even prayed with them for a cure. It does not come. Your prayers may seem unanswered.

This affliction, however, has not prevented the person from going on and having a very full life, even though they never received the healing they had so earnestly asked for. Sometimes, when a person comes into this world, there are certain lessons they are to learn. In order to learn, they must go through particular trials. Heavenly Father knows what is best for them and what they need in order to learn and grow. This is why He does not give them what they prayed for in the exact way that was requested. Their affliction may be an example to bolster someone else.

Imagine that you have just given your child a new bike. They are excited and want to go out and ride it right away, but you tell them not yet. First, they have to learn the safety rules and then they have to learn how to ride. Are you being thoughtless and not heading their pleas or are you lovingly helping them learn several lessons, like patience, importance of studying, and training?

At first, your child may be upset with you, but as you take their hand and lead and teach them what they need to know to be safe on their new bike, a bond will grow between you. They learn to rely on you and that you are always there for them. This is the way with Heavenly Father. He will lead you through the lessons you are to learn. He is always there and does hear every prayer. Sometimes He tells us no or that we must wait. "Faith always includes trust in God's timing." (Neal A. Maxwell)

No matter what your situation may be, always remember to keep your covenants with God. You may think He is not hearing your prayers or caring about you, but you are incorrect. Keeping your promises to Him and moving forward in faith is what you are meant to do. When you press forward in faith, you will be fortified against the adversary's attacks.

There is an old hymn that states," A mighty fortress is our God..." Fortresses have been erected down through the ages to protect against the invading hordes. There is usually a watch tower where a sentry keeps an eye out for the enemy. Our homes are fortresses from the evils of the world. We study and learn to come unto Christ and follow His commandments. By studying the scriptures together as a family when you can, and praying together, you are helping each other stay strong and on the right path. This is how you may become like Paul, "a new creature" with your hearts and minds in tune with God. You are going to need this to ward off the assaults of the adversary. It can be likened to putting on the "armor of God."

When you invite Christ into your life and home, you will feel a gentle guidance toward truth and peace. This bears witness that God lives and loves you. You will be inspired to live more worthily. All of this within the fortress of your humble home. Be aware that your home is only as strong as the faith of those within it.

"Watch ye therefore, and pray
always that ye may be accounted
worthy to escape these things
that shall come to pass..."

Luke 21:36

Concluding Thoughts for You to Consider

THE PRECEDING CHAPTERS HAVE GIVEN you information on how to detect if your soul or spirit is so wounded and sick that it is truly on life support. Tools and suggestions have been described and offered to help in the healing process. I hope that you have implemented them and found what you were seeking.

You have found out that the spirit can survive without the body, but the body cannot survive without the spirit. Just as you work to soften or avoid attacks on the body, it is important to protect the spirit from the assaults of the world. Acknowledge that things happen and take time to assess how you are really handling it.

One of the simplest, but at the same time, hardest ways to do that, is to invite the Lord into your life. You may say and think that you have invited the Lord in, but have you welcomed Him and made Him a priority like you would if you invited a dear friend in? Would you push your friend aside and go on with other tasks or would you take time to share and listen to them? Do you make the Lord first in your thoughts in the morning and last in the evening or do you only turn to Him when you are in need of something?

Learn to sincerely pray. Do it often. 1 Thessalonians 5:17 tells you to "Pray without ceasing." Start by thanking Him for the precious things that you have been given. Really take a minute and think about some of the blessings that you are grateful for. Be thankful.

Secondly: humbly and with your whole heart ask for what you feel in need of. Acknowledge that everything relies on His will, His way, and His timing. Do not try to give Him directions on how it should be done. End by thanking Him in the name of Jesus Christ.

Learn to listen and recognize His voice and guidance. Prayer is supposed to be a conversation with the Lord. The best conversations go both ways and are not one sided. Remember, always, that the Lord's will, way, and timing are perfect. He really does know the end from the beginning, and the beginning from the end. Sometimes you are told to wait. You may even be told 'No.' Trust that He has greater blessings for you down the road.

Blessings are not always what you may want or have asked for. They can come in various shapes, sizes and ways. Learn to look for them and be open to what happens. They are what the Lord wants for you and what is best for you.

Set aside a time each day to read and ponder the scriptures. The morning seems to work best for me. I am fresher and more open to learning. I have found answers to many things I sought in a line of scripture that I may have read dozens of times before and not recognized.

By studying the scriptures and praying often you will learn to recognize and then treasure each of the precious gifts and talents that you have been given so freely. Ponder these blessings and learn of your divine worth. You are a precious and special child of God. Keep that in mind and always remember it.

Life is not always exceedingly kind or loving. You may feel very isolated and unloved, and alone. Know that you are not alone. God is with you. The scriptures teach that He will never forsake you. Rest easy in this knowledge.

We learn from scripture to "love thy neighbor as thyself." Most people miss the second part of that commandment. They miss the "as thyself" part.

You must genuinely love yourself before you can love another fully. It means taking a little time to love that struggling soul within. Take a little time for yourself. Walk, read a book, engage in a hobby or learn a new one. Spend time with friends and loved ones. Learn to laugh like you were a child again.

Learn that it is okay to say "no" to some requests. Do it politely and with a smile. Stop feeling guilty about it for even a second. You do not have to take on every task that comes your way.

It is okay to not be 'okay' sometimes for a little bit. Allow yourself that freedom. Find a quiet place and yell, stomp your feet, or cry.

Do whatever makes you better. Ease up and stop striving for perfection every minute.

Love should be part of the foundation of your life—love of God, love of yourself, love of others. It feeds and heals you and your soul. In many ways, love is what makes life worth living. Without the light of love and loving, your soul withers. Open the window or door and let love enter.

Pray for guidance and move ahead whether you feel ready or not. Before long you will feel a lightening within you. That is your soul beginning to heal and grow strong again.

Rejoice in life and living. Offer love without expecting anything in return. You will receive much more than you expected. When you do not expect anything in return, you will be delighted by what comes back.

You are so very loved by your Heavenly Father. You are His precious child created in His own image. God loves you with His whole being. His arms are reaching out to hold you and heal you deep inside. You do truly deserve to learn of your divine worth.

Begin each day sincerely thanking God for the gift of another day and all the little and sometimes not so little blessings He sends into your life. There is an old hymn I sometimes hum to myself. It goes like this:

"Count your blessings.
Name them one by one.
Count your many blessings.
See what God has done."

He has never deserted you. You are generally just too busy to notice. Try unplugging from everything and really listen for that still, small voice inside you. Take delight in feeling the spirit of the Spirit. Learn to recognize it.

Whatever your personal trials may be, and we all have them, your Father in heaven is telling you that He loves you and will safely guide you if you but learn to listen and let Him.

Loving yourself is not a selfish act, like some may be feeling. By learning to sincerely love yourself, you will bring healing to your soul. You will find that you will be filled with a new strength and ability to love to the depths that you cannot imagine. Trust yourself. Love yourself.

Learn to act instead of reacting to things around you. There are times when anger is good. If you are fighting some injustice or for some cause, a little anger can be a benefit. Just do not let it become a way of life. Every warrior needs to lay down their sword sometime.

Pray and ask for God's help in releasing fear. Cease to be held captive by it. Claim your freedom from the cage it has put you in. Develop a testimony of faith, instead of a testimony of fear.

Fear of failure is one of the adversary's favorite weapons to use against us.

The only people who have not failed have not attempted much. Understand that you only fail when you do not get up again. Learn from your mistakes. That is all they are—lessons to be learned.

Your faith in Jesus Christ enables you to meet any challenge. It is similar to a suit of armor that shields you. With prayer and His guidance, you will find your way.

Now that your soul is healed, listen to its promptings and protect it. Just because it is healed does not mean that your soul does not need continued maintenance.

Hopefully, you have found some direction and purpose for yourself. Remember that your purpose can change as your life changes. Embrace the change and grow through it. Now is the time to create a beautiful masterpiece of your life.

I shall leave you with a quote from one of my favorite speakers.

"Create a masterpiece of your life. No matter our age, circumstances, or abilities, each one of us can create something remarkable of his life."

Joseph B. Wirthlin

About the Author

ALONG WITH HER HUSBAND, GEORGE, and two spoiled rescue dogs, Mary Gasa calls middle Michigan her home. Always working as a team , sharing their love of renovating and refurbishing, the couple's current project is giving new life to a two-story farmhouse built in 1905.

Mary believes in a strong bond that encompasses personal faith, spiritual and physical well-being that are cornerstones to a healthy life. She has earned a PhD in non-traditional nutrition from the American Holistic Health Academy. To add to her skills, she is a Reiki Master trained by Chikara – Reiki - Do and has become certified in the use of essential oils by sharing knowledge and inspiration, Mary has gained through the years is both a pleasure and a passion.

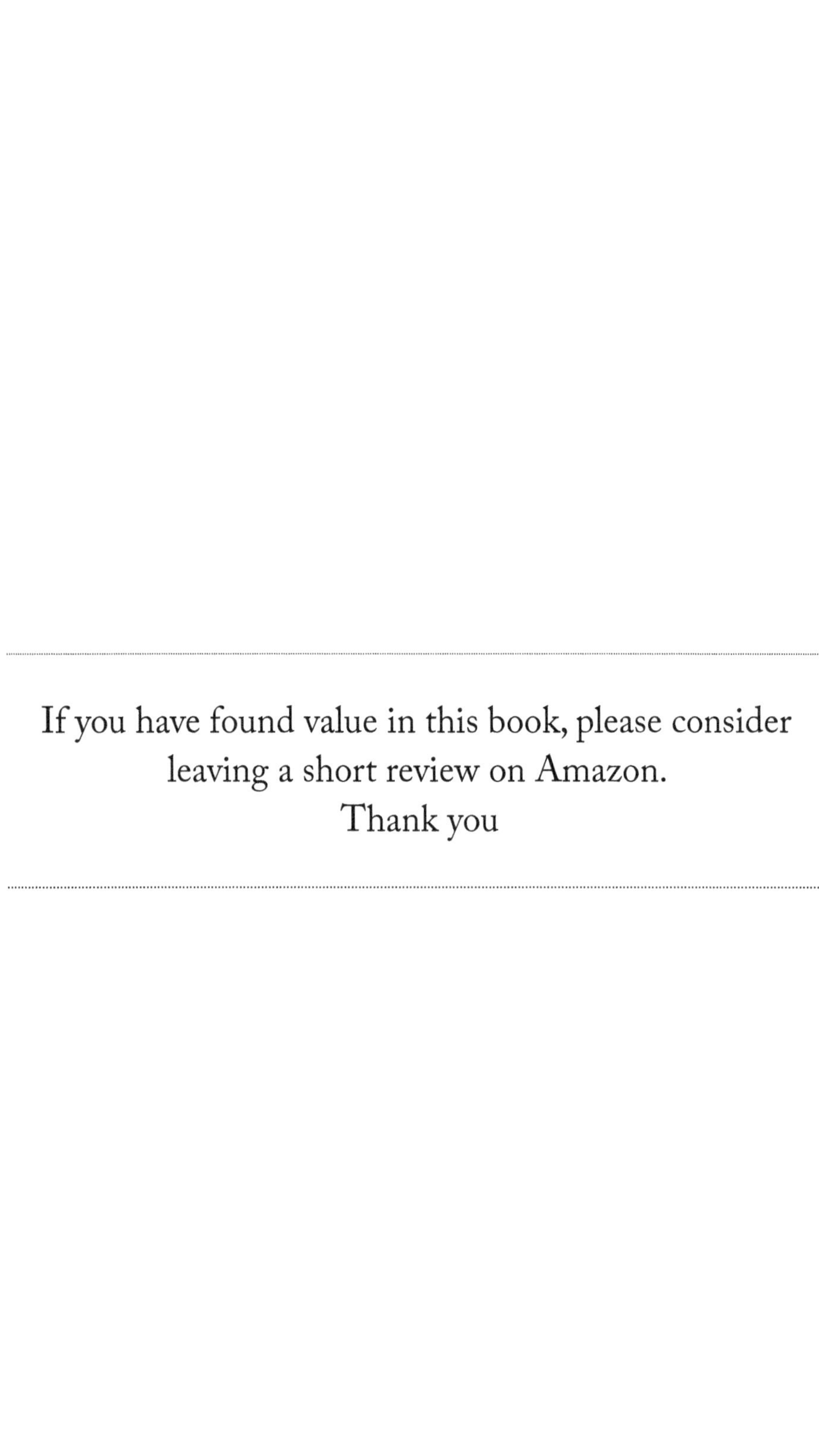
If you have found value in this book, please consider
leaving a short review on Amazon.
Thank you